750

Studies in Phenomenology

PHAENOMENOLOGICA

COLLECTION PUBLIÉE SOUS LE PATRONAGE DES CENTRES
D'ARCHIVES HUSSERL

30

DEBABRATA SINHA

Studies in Phenomenology

DEBABRATA SINHA

Studies in Phenomenology

MARTINUS NIJHOFF / THE HAGUE / 1969

PREFACE

The book is the result of my preoccupation with the phenomenological philosophy of Edmund Husserl during my years of post-doctoral studies (approximately since 1960). As the titles of the chapters may suggest, I have dealt with a number of topics relating to Husserlian Phenomenology – themes which are relatively independent but not disconnected. For I have been prone to look upon this movement as presenting more an organic outlook of its own, inspite of its diversity of phases, than as offering certain answers to individual philosophical problems. Accordingly my aim here has been to interpret the meaning and significance of this outlook in its logical, epistemological and metaphysical aspects.

In writing these chapters I have been aware of the fact that the phenomenological movement as such still represents something of a heterodoxy in the world of Anglo-American philosophy to-day. Yet the points of contact between the two are not far-fetched. In treating the problems from the phenomenological point of view, I have often taken into account the views of the empirical-analytical school in general.

It should be clear that instead of confining myself to a bare exposition of the different aspects of Husserlian Phenomenology, I have taken some freedom in interpreting its point of view. In my presentation of the latter, of course, I have tried to utilize the source materials in Husserl's works and relevant phenomenological literature. I lay no claim, however, to any final assessment of this type of philosophical thinking. I have sought only to bring into focus what appears to me to be its chief emphases, and to remove certain possible and actual misunderstandings regarding it. In fact I look upon Phenomenology as an open and expanding programme, which need not even wholly be identified with the original Husserlian aim of an absolutely presuppositionless philosophy, nor should terminate with the concluding phase of Husserlian thought.

I realize that there may be inadequacies in the present work arising from the fact that some material relating to recent investigations in the subject was not available in India. I have, however, received some useful books from Professor J. N. Mohanty (University of Burdwan, India).

As noted in relevant places, two chapters of this volume are in large reprinted or adapted (one in translation) from my previous publications in *Philosophy and Phenomenological Research* and *Zeitschrift für philosophische Forschung*. I am grateful to the editors of these two periodicals for their kind permission to make this further use of the material.

I gratefully acknowledge here the valuable assistance I have received from Professor Ludwig Landgrebe (University of Köln) and from Professor Walter Biemel (University of Aachen) in connection with my studies in this field. To Rev. Prof. H. L. Van Breda (Louvain) I owe a debt of gratitude for his kind interest in my works. I should also acknowledge the kind co-operation from Professor Marvin Farber (State University of New York at Buffalo) and from Professor Herbert Spiegelberg (Washington University). Finally I take this opportunity of expressing my thankfulness to the president and members of the Board of Editors of this series, and to Martinus Nijhoff, the publishers of this volume.

Calcutta, February, 1968   DEBABRATA SINHA

CONTENTS

CHAPTER I

INTRODUCTION

I. *Philosophy as Critique of Experience*

1.1 A standing problem in philosophy is the problem of relating the empirical with what is supposed to transcend experience. But the problem of transcendence in relation to experience – in other words, the relation of the empirical with the trans-empirical – seems to take a particularly acute shape in modern non-speculative philosophy, or Critical philosophy since Kant. Not prepossessed by the task of constructing a metaphysical system of "First Principles", critical philosophy at large has been, in one way or other, preoccupied with the major problem of establishing a necessary link between the empirical and the non-empirical. The latter, however, is not *a priori* posited as the realm of supersensible realities. For critical philosophy would depend neither on pure rationalizing nor on deductive procedure out of certain postulates and general principles.

1.2 So a type of philosophy, which is not otherwise preoccupied with metaphysical questions, poses for itself the problem of criticism of experience. Unhindered by metaphysical presuppositions, it takes as its point of departure the very stratum of experience itself. But the interest here is not in any way confined to the psychological explanation of the states of experience nor to a natural-scientific explanation of the objective order of things. The interest is, on the contrary, primarily *epistemological*, i.e., directed to the sphere of knowing itself. The concern for analysis of knowledge and experience is precisely one pertaining to the conditions for the possibility of knowledge and experience.

1.3 Thus we come to the problematic of what is known as *transcendental* philosophy. The clue to the concept of "transcendental" (as distinguished from "transcendent") can be traced from the philosophy of Kant. The transcendental is not only not given to experience, but it is also necessarily presupposed by experience. In this sense the concept provides the guiding motive in the phenomenological philosophy of Edmund Husserl. As he proposes it, the problematic of phenomenological philosophy – or of "transcendental phenomenology", as he later prefers to designate it – is to trace back the final source in which all possible forms of knowledge are functionally grounded.

1.4 From the said transcendental motive in philosophizing the idea of presuppositionless philosophy is not far removed. A philosophy, which is to investigate into the preconditions making knowledge possible, cannot itself accept presuppositions – to be consistent in its critical procedure. So a philosophy, free from presuppositions, should alone be competent to probe into the presuppositions themselves implied by knowledge and experience. The possible presupposition for a philosophic endeavour may be introduced at two levels – that of the naïvely posited facts and existents, and of the metaphysical level of transcendent unconditioned reality (or realities). As for phenomenology, it proposes to steer clear of both the ends of "naturalistic" (as the typical Husserlian expression puts it) as well as of higher-level metaphysical commitments.

II. *Phenomenological Program*

2.1 The idea of presuppositionless philosophy serves as the target in the new philosophical discipline of phenomenology. This aim of freedom from possible presuppositions – metaphysical or otherwise – is, of course, not absolutely new in philosophy. For as early as Aristotle, there had been prevailing the conception of "first philosophy" (cf. "Erste Philosophie" – a title of Husserl's work). Descartes also wanted to build up his philosophy free from beliefs and presuppositions. Husserl only took up the idea more radically and rigorously – on firm methodological principles, introducing altogether a fresh line of investigations.

2.2 Indeed in proposing a radical program of a new philosophical discipline, which should be at the same time free from presuppositions, Husserl poses a root question – or a "question backwards" *(Rückfrage)*, as he puts it. This means, in other words, turning from experience back to the foundational sources out of which the forms of knowledge – of both scientific as well as prescientific types – arise. So the task before phenomenology is to treat genetic questions regarding the foundations of meaning which constitute the framework of science and philosophy. Phenomenology is not ready to stop with the naive acceptance of the reality of things, but proposes to probe into the roots of objectivity, i.e., into the respective essences constituting the meaning of the objects in view. As the Husserlian motto typically declares, the movement of phenomenological analysis should be "back to things themselves" *(zu den Sachen selbst)*. ["Things" here referred to are not, of course, *real* objects but the elements which are phenomenologically evident – a point discussed in the following essays.]

2.3 Once this radical question regarding the ultimate foundations of knowledge is posed, a demand for remodelling the very idea of philosophical system has to be recognized. Accordingly Husserl put forward his program for a total reform of philosophical discipline, shaping philosophy into rigorous science. Indeed Husserl put forward, at the early stage of his philosophical career, the ideal of his program: philosophy as rigorous science *(Philosophie als strenge Wissenschaft)*.[1] This ideal almost reflected an adherence to the Cartesian conception of grounding philosophy on the model of mathematical knowledge – in point of certainty and exactitude. If philosophy is to gain the certainty of knowledge pertaining to exact sciences, Husserl urges, it should be entirely based on "evidence" in reflecting consciousness. Phenomenological philosophy, it is urged, should be nothing less and nothing more than a system of indubitable statements based on strict evidence. And the evidence in view is to be derived from what is called "intuition" *(Anschauung)* in the phenomenological context.

2.4 However much phenomenology may approach the ideal of scientific knowledge, yielding certain truths, it yet hardly

---

[1] Cf. Husserl's article in *Logos*, 1910: "Philosophie als strenge Wissenschaft".

represents a typical case of a philosophical system or doctrine in
the strict sense. And this is a feature, among ohters, that distinguishes phenomenology from such systems as Cartesianism,
which also lay claim to a strictly scientific character. That is
because phenomenology concerns itself with the methodological
outlook and standpoint rather than with a group of determinate
truths concerning things. Its interest lies in the way of analysis
rather than in the theory of being. In that sense, phenomenology
is hardly entitled to be called a close-knit school of thinking,
although it is certainly more than a mere philosophical tendency
or a style of philosophizing. It is in broad a new philosophical
discipline, offering its own methodology and standpoint in the
understanding of knowledge and experience. And its outlook is
defined and elaborated in the development of the phenomenological movement itself, and not *ab initio* determined in an *a priori*
manner.

III.   *Beyond Empiricism*

3.1 A critique of experience need not mean philosophical
empiricism. To take a first-hand view of experinece in the explanation of knowledge does not imply that such explanation has
to move within the *empirical* frame of reference alone. One is apt
to recall here the familiar Kantian formula: all our knowledge
begins with experience but does not arise out of experience.[2]
Even if metaphysical presuppositions are not brought in, an
attempt towards a complete explanation of knowledge need not
proceed in terms of contents of sense experience. An attempt to
put forward a thoroughly empirical foundation of knowledge is
likely to lead either to a sceptical conclusion – as conspicuously
in the case of Humean empiricism – or to some sort of linguistic
formalism – as in modern analytical positivistic thinking. In one
case we find a futile attempt to bridge the gulf between experience
and knowledge; in the other, it is more a formalist rendering of
experience in terms of propositions subject to empirical verification, and not directly an account of experience.

---

[2] Cf. "Wenn aber gleich alle unsere Erkenntnis mit der Erfahrung anhebt, so
entspringt sie darum doch nicht eben alle aus der Erfahrung." – Kant, *Kritik der
reinen Vernunft* (2. Ausgabe), *Einleitung* 1.

3.2 Now experience, in all possible stages of presentation, readily reveals certain generalities, which are themselves not derived or derivable from experience. Thus universal concepts or categories come into play in the role of organizing experience – employed as presuppositions, involved within the structure of experience. The *general* character of these concepts is, however, not to be referred to experience, i.e., not derived through empirical generalization. For the latter can yield only probability, and cannot certify that necessity which is required of those principles, if they are to serve in organizing experience. In brief, a search for the empirical basis of generalities can hardly bear fruitful results.

3.3 This leads on to the question of non-empirical (or rather, over-empirical) status of such general concepts. They cannot be regarded as *facts* of higher generality, secured through generalization from particular facts. Rather a fact-neutral status has to be granted to them, having yet a necessary bearing on experience – in other words, an *ideal* status which should be non-factual (and to that extent, non-real), but nevertheless presuppositional. Accordingly the approach to such alleged principles would differ from a mere empirical approach to the given, as much as from a purely metaphysical one. A kind of "intuition" may be spoken of, but only with regard to the idealities concerned. As such it is to be distinguished from the intuition of the sensibly evident, i.e., empirical intuition, on the one hand, and metaphysical intuition of supersensible reality (or realities) on the other.[3]

3.4 The phenomenological way of thinking thus sharply departs from the empirical-positivist tradition in the explanation of knowledge. It would not agree to confine its analysis to sense-data language, or to associations of "atomic" mental states – as conspicuously in the philosophy of David Hume. A reduction to either of them – to psychological determination of the elemental states of consciousness or to elementary sense-data statements – would be, from the phenomenological point of view, a reduction in the wrong direction. Of course, the phenomenologist seems *prima facie* to share the positivist attitude of recognizing the given in experience towards forming a system of knowledge. But

---

[3] Intuition in the former sense is illustrated, for example, in the Kantian use of the expression *Anschauung* (in "Transcendental Aesthetic" in his first Critique), and the latter in the general tradition of metaphysical philosophy – in some form or other.

the definition of the given and its scope would differ entirely in the two philosophies concerned. Phenomenology seeks to overrule the limits laid down by the empiricist tradition at large – viz., those of sense preception – and of psychological atomism connected therewith. One might be prompted to regard phenomenology as a higher-order positivism – or more appropriately, as "transcendental positivism".

[See Chapter II: "Phenomenology and the Empiricist Tradition"].

IV. *New Method: New Logic*

4.1 So not being confined within the limits of empiricist commitment to sense-data and yet ready to submit to the direct evidence of consciousness, phenomenology has to make out its own method of investigation. The need for method was particularly felt by those philosophers of the modern age who attempted to establish their respective views on firm foundations of knowledge – philosophers like Descartes and Kant, among others. As to non-speculative philosophers, Hume had already been methodologically conscious; only he shifted the question to psychological directions. Now Husserl's program for a presuppositionless philosophy, probing into presuppositions themselves, calls for a new method in the analysis and interpretation of experience. While departing from the empiricist approach in terms of psychologistic reduction to mental elements and/or inductive generalization, phenomenology would not at the same time depend on purely formal-analytical procedure.

4.2 Indeed methodology has been one great concern in phenomenological philosophy – aiming as it does at absolutely certain truths, which should nevertheless be free from reference to real being. Accordingly arises a need for new logic, a new way of reasoning, adjusted to the task of linking experience to the over-empirical. Kant in his Critical philosophy had already anticipated a "transcendental logic",[4] a transcendental method, which, though not substituting formal logic, should be a significant addition to it. Methodologically more keenly aware than

---

[4] Cf. "Transzendentale Elementarlehre", 2. Teil, *Kritik der reinen Vernunft.*

Kant, Husserl took up the clue from Kantian transcendental logic, but worked out its methodological implications with greater rigour and thoroughness.

4.3 The aim of phenomenological procedure is to bring the intuitive element of the given and the *a priori* element into harmony. But phenomenology would evidently not fall in line with the two logics usually pertaining to the respective spheres of empirical induction and formal deduction. Induction yielding probability cannot justify the genuinely *a priori* status of the logical concepts and laws. On the other hand, pure formal logic, i.e., logic pertaining to the formal *a priori*, is hardly competent to provide the *modus operandi* along which the *a priori* implicates could be traced behind the level of the empirically given. The problem of bringing the alleged apriorities (or idealities) within the range of evidence – non-empirical non-factual though the latter may be – would arise, if the whole situation is looked at from the phenomenological point of view. Accordingly transcendental logic comes into play, promising a new level of reasoning in sharp distinction from the traditional formal-objective logic. [See Chapter III: "Critique of Formal Logic"].

V. *Turn to Subjectivity*

5.1 Unlike common formal-logical reasoning, the so-called "transcendental logic" or transcendental method of philosophizing proceeds from experience back to presuppositions, and not *vice versa*. In that way the alleged presuppositions present themselves as essentially related to the cognizing consciousness itself. Indeed the *raison d'être* of logical and metaphysical apriorities lie in the originating functionality of consciousness or subjectivity. Consequently a pursuit of the transcendental method calls for a shifting from the formal-objective attitude to the subjective level of knowing or the level of subjective orientation in knowing. To put it simply, the phenomenological mode of interpretation proceeds not from the object that is known but rather from the way in which our knowledge of object is obtained. (One is reminded here of the so-called "Copernican" standpoint in Kantianism.)

5.2 But the phenomenological concern for subjectivity – in

neglect of object or objective reality (though not of objectivity, i.e., the presentation of object to reflecting consciousness) – is apt to be misunderstood as a preference for a psychologically oriented theory of knowledge. So the crux of the problem lies with the definition of subjectivity in the genuinely phenomenological context. Is the phenomenological method of positing idealities on the basis of what is evident in intuition, vitiated by narrow psychological subjectivism? Moreover, should consciousness – to which all modes of objectivity are sought to be reduced – be understood in psychological terms? So the charge has to be met if phenomenology, in its method outlook and conclusions, does imply subjectivism (in the narrow psychological sense).

[See Chapter IV: "Subjectivism in Phenomenology"].

5.3 Phenomenology, of course, has its own positive concept of subjectivity. As providing the frame of reference within which all meaning of objectivity are formed, subjectivity can be looked upon as the precondition of all analysis of objectivity. How, then, is the nature of such subjectivity to be defined else than as the presupposition for all explanation? In fact the concept of "transcendental subjectivity" points to that presuppositional functional status. On ultimate analysis, "transcendental subjectivity" proves to be a final term of reference which cannot further be reduced in phenomenological terms. But the question may still arise: is subjectivity (or consciousness) to be understood as nothing more than a nominal expression or a blanket-term? (See Ch. IV).

5.4 The problem of subjectivity can be viewed from another aspect too, viz., that of a concrete human person. There the question would arise: how to relate the fundamental concept of subjectivity, the supposed principle of universal explanation, to the real complex which is ordinarily referred to as *person* (denoted in another way as *ego*)? For subjectivity (i.e., consciousness) is *prima facie* intelligible in the context of human individual or person. A phenomenological analysis of the area of phenomena called *personal*, i.e., connected with person, is therefore of particular significance for an understanding of phenomenological philosophy. The orientation of the concept of person in phenomenology has therefore to be taken into consideration for understanding the real nature and place of subjectivity in that system. [See Chapter V: "Concept of Person and Subjectivity" (where the actual method of phenomenological investigation is sought to be exemplified, with reference to a significant sphere of being, viz., human person – one that lies closest, so to say, to the underlying principle of subjectivity)].

VI. *Interpretation of Science*

6.1 The phenomenologist's preoccupation with subjectivity and his explanation of objectivity essentially in the light of that do not, however, cancel the basically *descriptive* character of phenomenology. Of course, "description" in the phenomenological sense would not pertain to facts and events but rather to reality-neutral essentialities as evident in the region of reflecting consciousness. Accordingly the phenomenological method of investigations should have access to all possible fields of experience. And in this approach phenomenology no doubt shares a point of contact with the general procedure of natural sciences, though it does not itself offer to be a science, nor a substitute for it.

6.2 The analysis of the rationale of natural science – its *modus operandi* and conceptual framework – is indeed one of the chief concerns of phenomenological philosophy. So the problem in connection with the foundation of scientific knowledge is sought to be dealt with on the line of phenomenological analysis of the structure of that knowledge. Accordingly the process of formation of the concepts employed in scientific theory has to be reviewed in the light of their origin in the functionality of consciousness. Here again a phenomenological philosophy of science – so far as it can possibly be represented – has to meet the claim of the alternative explanation of scientific knowledge, put forward in the positivistically oriented philosophy of science – particularly the phenomenalist point of view.

6.3 Beyond methodological criticism, phenomenology offers further a basic critique of the very *raison d'être* of positive science on its theoretic level. Thus abstraction is regarded as the keynote to the development of the mathematically-oriented theoretic superstructure of natural science. Consequent upon this abstraction there is estrangement of scientific theory from the stratum of common experience of life. The so-called objectivity of positive sciences – otherwise held to be their greatest virtue – is found, on analysis, to betray the basic shortcoming of science inherent in its method and outlook.

6.4 With its acclaimed universal method of transcendental analysis, phenomenology is ready to meet the critical situation (Husserl calls it "crisis") brought about through the said abstractionism. The positive way of recovery from this situation, as Husserl recommends, is a turn back to the primary world of common experience preceding science. And it is not an arbitrary movement. For, if the hidden meaning of the theoretic constructions of science is to be restored, a link has to be established with the foundations of subjectivity – unless, of course, we choose not to question the meaning of the theoretic-abstract framework of natural science. Now, where could we search for this bridge else than in some potential field of subjectivity where sophisticated concepts have not yet come into operation? And Husserl points to the world of prescientific experience – he calls it the "world of life" *(Lebenswelt)* – as the basic stratum, out of which all the meaning-contents proceed to constitute subsequent concepts. Hence the cardinal significance of the world of life in the phenomenological examination of the foundations of science – nay, of all possible knowledge. Thus the earlier dictum of phenomenology, *"zu den Sachen"*, gives place to the motto: back to experience.

[See Chap. VI: "Phenomenology as Philosophy of Science"].

VII. *The Metaphysical Question*

7.1 One lingering question remains all through the phenomenological investigations – it is the question of reality. Its interest centered around first-hand analysis of the evident in experience, phenomenology is avowedly non-metaphysical. It can at best be considered as "metaphysic of experience" (in the Kantian way) – though an open system for that – and not as a metaphysics of reality. Whether as philosophy of consciousness or as philosophy of science, phenomenology offers a metaphysically non-committal position, so far as its concern is with the "meaning of being" rather than with being as such – with idealities presupposed in experience rather than with realities postulated in theory. For a commitment on the metaphysical question of reality – be it at the natural level or at the supersensible level – would no doubt be in the way of a truly presuppositionless enquiry.

7.2 Yet phenomenological investigations – at certain points – seem to verge on metaphysical issues. Though not directly aiming at a theory of reality or a theory of Being, it is doubtful whether the ontological question concerning the nature of being as such can be avoided in the long run. Is not some ontological implication there, even for the idealities concerned? Are the essences, pertaining to different regions of experience, intelligible entirely by themselves apart from the reality context? There seems to be an attempt on phenomenological lines towards a reconciliation between the two levels – essence-level and reality-level – in the shape of the so-called "regional ontologies".

[See Chapter VII: "Is Phenomenology Ontologically Committed?"]

7.3 This question of ontological status presents itself with particular urgency in connection with the acclaimed foundational principle of phenomenological explanation, i.e., transcendental subjectivity or consciousness. The concept of pure consciousness, referred to as autonomous region and home of all meaning, brings into relief the question concerning its reality. Could such principle remain foundational without having a reality status of its own? On closer examination it may seem that phenomenology hovers between the metaphysical demand and the phenomenological neutrality in the strict sense, so far as the question of the reality of consciousness is concerned. [See Chap. VII].

7.4 Phenomenology no doubt offers to work out afresh a philosophy on rigorous lines of analysis, free from metaphysical commitment. At least no easy metaphysical commitment or theorization seems to affect the phenomenological procedure – an ideal which as such is no doubt hard to pursue in philosophizing. It can be pointed out, however, that a direction towards a metaphysical world-view can be found present in phenomenological philosophy taken as a whole. What could possibly be kept an open question in the path of phenomenological investigations seems to yield in the long run to a potent metaphysical drive for a teleologically oriented idealistic metaphysics. And that perhaps marks the point where, it seems, strict phenomenological limits have been outstepped. [See Ch. VIII, 6.]

CHAPTER II

PHENOMENOLOGY AND THE EMPIRICIST TRADITION[1]

I

The central point of positivism – taking "positivism" in the wider sense of empirical philosophy at large – is the emphasis on the *given* in the interpretation of knowledge. All knowledge, according to empirical-positivistic philosophy in general, is based on the sense-given as the real source of knowledge. Positivism thus tends to be a philosophy of the given – one that seeks to base all systems of knowledge, free from presuppositions, on the *positive*, i.e., on what is actually and originally given in consciousness. In this sense, Husserl claims, phenomenology would amount to positivism; referring to the common point in view, he remarks: ". . . then we are genuine positivists".[2]

As a matter of methodological principle, phenomenology refers back to "evidence". What it accepts as the "source of authority" *(Rechtsquelle)* for all rational statements is immediate "seeing" *(Sehen)* – not the bare seeing of sensuous experience, but seeing in the sense of originally given consciousness. Husserl formulates "the principle of all principles" in these words: "Every type of first-hand intuiting forms a legitimate source of authority; whatever presents itself in intuition at first hand – bodily present, as it were – is to be accepted simply as it presents itself, though within the limits of its presentation".[3]

To understand properly the role of the said "intuition" *(An-*

[1] Adapted from the author's article: "Phenomenology and Positivism", pub. in *Philosophy and Phenomenological Research*, June 1963.
[2] "Sagt Positivismus so viel wie absolut vorurteilfreie Gründung aller Wissenschaften auf das 'Positive', das originär zu Erfassende, dann sind wir die echten Positivisten." – Husserl, *Ideen* I, § 20.
[3] *Ibid*, § 24.

schauung), the phenomenological way of thinking itself has to be taken into consideration. The latter proceeds by way of "bracketing" *(Einklammerung)* the natural belief in the existential reality of the world of facts. As conditioned by such "bracketing" ,facts are to be viewed not qua facts but as "phenomena", i.e., as object-meanings (not actual objects as such), which are obtained through the neutralizing of the factual character of objects.[4]

To state the Husserlian principle in another way, the methodological reference to the self-givenness of the content in intuition would hardly leave room for a deductive search for such constructions as are unrelated to the content in view. The method and aim should be, on the contrary, to derive all knowledge from final sources, i.e., from the principles which present themselves in and through insight *(selbstgesehenen eingesehenen Prinzipien)*. In that sense the phenomenological procedure is not to be diverted by any prejudice nor by any verbal construction – indeed by nothing in the world, not even what goes by the name of "exact science". It should, on the contrary, accept the right of whatever is clearly seen – that which constitutes the "original" in consciousness, preceding all theories and ultimately setting all norms for explanation.[5]

As for the principle of givenness, however, Husserl's phenomenology is preceded by the tradition of empiricism and positivism. But the distinction on this point in respect of the two movements is chiefly determined by the interpretation of this very element of givenness. Even the Husserlian "principle of all principles" does not make it adequately clear as to what exactly constitutes the immediately given or intuited at first hand. The *given* may range from the bare sense-given, i.e., the data of sensuous intuition, to the highest possible limit of *ideal* generalities of thought. Phenomenology seems to share the positivist-empiricist denial of ideal constructions or of metaphysical presuppositions and theories; these are all beyond the range of the given. Nevertheless the "given" has a far wider scope for phenomenology than in positivism.

[4] Cf. E. Fink speaks of the "methodically exercised neutralization of the asserted character" of objects – ". . . Gegenstandssinn bei methodisch geübter Neutralisierung der thetischen Charaktere". Vide Fink, "Operative Begriffe in Husserls Phäno-menologie" in *Zeitschrift für philosophische Forschung*, XI, 1957.
[5] Vide "Entwurf einer Vorrede zu den 'Logischen Untersuchungen'" (1913), ed. by E. Fink in *Tijdschrift voor Philosophie*, I (1939), § 3.

Here arises the question whether the ideal generalities recognized in phenomenology, i.e., essences or essentialities, can
be taken as *given* in the strict sense of the expression. Phenomenology would certainly not agree with positivism in restricting
givenness to the experienced particular alone, and in rejecting
the possibility of an intuition of general essences and idealities.
According to Husserl, the positivists are prejudiced in not accepting anything other than particular data or sense-data.
Empiricism generally presupposes that only the individual sense-
particular can be originally given. The denial of the possibility
of intuitive comprehension of universals as such is, of course,
accompanied by the denial of the possible *(ideal)* being of
universals in the form of "essences".

In his critique of empirical philosophy Husserl shows how the
denial of ideal generalities in knowledge could imply deeper
contradiction within the framework of empirical theory of
knowledge itself.[6] Thus, to begin with Locke, his doctrine of
"general ideas", his theory of intuitive and demonstrative knowledge, and his recognition that pure mathematics and pure morals
are founded on intuition and demonstration – all these manifestly
contradict the empiricist standpoint itself. Locke seeks to present
an epistemological foundation of the objectivity of positive science
through psychological investigations. This was effected in terms
of his sensualistic position concerning the data of knowledge
derived from outer and inner senses. Sensualism remains the basis
of Locke's psychologically oriented theory of knowledge; the
only indubitable basis of all knowledge is, on ultimate analysis, to
be found in the experience of self and its region of immanent data.
From the standpoint of what Husserl calls the "sensationalism of
data", Locke offers his theory of abstractionism in the form of
"general ideas" constructed out of particular data of outer and
inner sense.

As against Locke's theory of abstraction, Husserl argues that
general essentialities *(Wesenheiten)* are objects, or rather meant
as objects, in consciousness. As individual contents they are

---

[6] In his last work, *Die Krisis der europäischen Wissenschaften und die transzendentale
Phänomenologie* (secs. 22ff.), Husserl critically reviews the development of British
empirical philosophy from Locke to Hume in particular, in his attempt to assign
the place of phenomenological philosophy in the larger perspective of modern
European thought.

unities in manifold consciousness, which means them. And Husserl contends that immediate self-comprehension *(Selbst-erfassung)* of such contents of a special kind as the essences is an evident possibility, so far as they present themselves in consciousness as *intending objects*. Husserl, however, anticipates the possible objections that may be raised against his own thesis concerning general essentialities. Thinking, after all, is a mediate consciousness, while intuition is immediate. The latter implies passivity, grasping in a given, while thinking is manifold activity going out of the given. But to this it is pointed out by Husserl that even passivity presents manifold implications within itself, in spite of its immediacy; similarly in the case of thinking activity too, heterogenous shades may be detected on closer examination. The whole range of active synthesis may constitute the unity of self-giving in thought. So Husserl suggests that the idea of "intuition" *(Anschauung)* should be broadened so as to bring within its range not merely sense particulars but also – and more significantly – the *ideal* concepts and types.

In this respect Husserl criticizes empiricism – particularly of the Lockean form – as only a half-way intuitionism or apparent empiricism *(Scheinempirismus)*. For in the latter the empiricist principle of going back upon experience – the content viewing itself – is only partly worked out, and not in its fuller consistency. Although Locke started with the idea of inner-psychological investigations, he failed to grasp the idea of an "eidetic science of pure consciousness" – one that phenomenology aims at.[7]

In a different context, in his *"Logische Untersuchungen"*, Husserl had already shown the inadequacy of a purely psychological basis for ideal laws *("Idealgesetze"* as distinguished from *"Realgesetze")*. He argues that psychology cannot give more than empirical universals as generalizations from psychical phenomena and dispositions and organic processes. That is why psychology cannot yield apodictically evident, over-empirical and exact laws which constitute the core of all logic.[8]

---

[7] Husserl, *Erste Philosophie*, Vol. I, sec. 19.
[8] See Chap. III (6), for Husserl's criticism of "psychologism" – particularly in his *Logical Investigations*.

II

The distinction of Husserlian Phenomenology from the empirical-positivist philosophy of David Hume is particularly worth noting. Hume draws the empiricist direction of Locke to its further radical conclusion. Already Berkeley had carried the sensationalism, embedded in Locke's psychological orientation of the theory of knowledge, towards a nominalistic direction; Hume developed it in the shape of atomistic psychology. For Hume, all beings, bodily as well as mental, reduce themselves to elementary psychical data, to the mass of perceptions not integrated to any "I". In terms of atoms of consciousness' all contents of experience are to be explained; and corresponding to the laws of the external world, the inner laws of association and habit are there. Consequently, the whole world with all its objectivity is sought to be reduced to a system of apparent forms or "fictions" which takes its rise in subjectivity according to immanent laws of the mental life. Thus a "fictionalistic epistemology" naturally springs from Hume's psychology; all categories of objectivity are shown to be nothing but "fictions".

So far as the sceptical attitude towards the objective world of science – or as Husserl puts it, "objectivism" of science in general – is concerned, Husserl would in a sense join issue with Hume. Husserl, like Hume, questions the objective validity of the world of science. But while Hume, in his scepticism, would not go further than the common categories of objective explanation, such as causality, substance etc., Husserl fixes his attention more on the mathematico-physical construction upon the given world of common experience. Husserl is not against the validity of the scientific world as such, but he points out emphatically the disconnection of such an abstracted scientific explanation from the concrete world of common experience – as Husserl calls it, the prescientific "life-world" *(Lebenswelt)*.[9] So, unlike Hume, Husserl does not examine the commonly accepted categories of science as such, but he rather reviews the whole attempt of the Galilean and the succeeding physical science which proceeded by constructing theoretico-logical superstructures in place of the world of living experience.

[9] See *infra*, Chap. VI regarding Husserl's critique of science.

None the less Husserl subjects Humeanism to sharp criticism even from within. According to him, Hume and the succeeding empiricists turn impressions and ideas, admittedly the only two elements of consciousness, into material signs *(sachliche Merkmale)*. This attribution of the thing-character (though of the psychical type) vitiates the Humean distinction between impressions and ideas, and the primacy of impressions. So far as my consciousness, stands for the region of what is immediately evident, the distinction of impressions and ideas may suggest a bare distinction of two types of things. Actually a confusion is there as to the dual aspects of "impression" – their evidencing and entitative characters. On the one hand, impression is looked upon as a *thing* and as such sought to be described through the use of material sign. It is, on the other hand, taken to be the experience itself of the self-given content experienced. Now bare things exist without signifying or meaning anything. But for Hume impressions are the epistemological title for that intuition which is competent to serve in the acts of consciousness as the verification of evidence. But a *thing* as such cannot verify anything; only the evidencing of something in its self-presentation – in the phenomenological language, "self-intuition" *(Selbstanschauung)* – be it in perceiving or remembering or otherwise, can verify or certify.

Husserl further seeks to show inconsistency in the inductive-empirical objectivism as demonstrated in Hume's theory. The fundamental attempt to bring facts of inner experience under empirical inductive laws threatens to reduce the sphere of consciousness to one of unreason or *probability;* for according to Humean empiricism itself, there can be no absolute reason for the validity of bare empirical laws. On the one hand, the Humean psychology of atomism and associationism is meant to be an objectively valid science, which again, on Hume's own admission, serves as the foundation of all possible knowledge. But to follow the Humean analysis concerning science as such, this psychology itself has, after all, to be treated as only subjectively grounded – and to that extent, other than *objective* psychology. Here lies a fundamental anomaly in the Humean theory.

A further contradiction – and a fundamental one – in Humeanism is thus pointed out by Husserl: "The whole construction of Humean scepticism as a theory which seeks to demonstrate all reality and all science of reality as fiction, becomes possible only through a kind of intellectual dishonesty".[10] On the one hand, Hume recognizes the rational truth of the relation of causality – in fact, the explanation of this rationality is his problem. On the other hand, the final thesis of Humeanism maintains the unreasonableness of the principle so far as it is not warranted by the verdict of immediate experience in the form of "impressions".

Consequently, Husserl declares, Humean scepticism ends in the "bankruptcy" of philosophy itself – indeed, of all systematic knowledge about the world. It proves to be the "bankruptcy of objective knowledge" – "ein Bankrott der objektiven Erkenntnis".[11] In this fate of Humeanism, again, Husserl discovers an evident contradiction. For philosophy demonstrates that all sciences of facts are, on ultimate analysis, unreasonable (i.e., probable). On the other hand, philosophy, so far as it is nothing but universal psychology for Hume, should itself be treated as a "science of facts".

To be strictly consistent, the very assertion that universal categories and their comprehension are merely subjective fictions, proves to be itself self-defeating. For the (general) statement regarding "fictions" should then be treated as nothing but a *probable* one – no guarantee for the objectivity of a general probable statement being admittedly there. Now, the Humean standpoint on probability is subjected to criticism in the light of phenomenological analysis. In the *psychological* analysis of universal experiential statements, which necessarily are probability statements, the rationale – which is otherwise to be phenomenologically grasped within the region of "relations of ideas" – is missed. Husserl would refer a probability statement rather to its corresponding evidence in the original experience *(Empirie)* – "the evidence of probability statement" *(die Evidenz der Wahrscheinlichkeitsbehauptung)*, from which the ideal possibility pertaining to the objective validity of laws is ultimately obtained.[12]

---

10 *Erste Philosophie*, Vol. I, § 25.
11 *Die Krisis* etc., § 23.
12 Vide *Erfahrung und Urteil*, Beilage II, p. 472ff. Also see below, Ch. VI, 4.
  N.B. Even the Humean illustration of die-throw is interpreted by Husserl in the line of phenomenological evidence. Thus the so-called probability pertaining to each statement on the throw acquires, so to say, an "weight" obtained from earlier grounds of experience *(Erfahrungsgründe)*. *Ibid*, p. 476.

III

In Humean scepticism, however, Husserl still finds a precursor of phenomenological philosophy. For Hume's positivism not only marked the completion of the sceptical attitude but also the decisive step towards a "fundamental science" *(Grundwissenschaft)*, which is *transcendental* in character. The sensationalistic subjectivism of Hume makes for an evidence-oriented immanental philosophy, and anticipates to that extent a genuinely "intuitionistic" philosophy such as phenomenology proposes to be. Husserl in fact admits that Hume's "Treatise" presents the first systematic sketch of what phenomenology might be – although it actually took the reverse direction of sensationalism.[13]

The most significant step towards the development of what may be called "transcendental subjectivism" – which found clearer formulation in Kantian philosophy – can be traced in Humeanism, though implicitly. For the far-reaching results of empirical scepticism was clearly and unambiguously to notice what was already implied in Cartesianism, namely, that the whole knowledge of the world – prescientific as well as scientific – is fundamentally of the nature of a "riddle". Already with Descartes, the immanent faculty of sensibility was taken to produce pictures of the world. With Berkeley, this sensuous character of knowledge is extended much further to cover the very world of bodies. And with Hume, it is the mind in its totality – constituted of impressions and ideas, along with the laws of association and the faculty of "imagination" – which produces the whole world itself as obtained in rational science as well as in common experience. This "production", however, is nothing more than a fiction, a representation which is innerly determined. Thus through the regeneration and radicalization of the fundamental problem of Cartesianism in the philosophy of Berkeley, and more decidedly in that of Hume, "dogmatic" objectivism was shaken to its core. And it was not only the contemporary mathematical objectivism which attributed to the world a mathematical-rational self-

---

[13] Cf. Husserl, "Nachwort zu meinen *Ideen zu einer reinen Phänomenologie und phänomenologischen Philosophie*", *Jahrbuch für Philosophie und phänomenologische Forschung*, Bd. XI (1930).

subsistence,[14] but the objectivism in general which had been coming down through a century or more.

The fundamental problem of Hume was to make intelligible the naively accepted certainty of the world as a matter of fact. Once Hume had discerned that the world is one constructed in subjectivity, the so-called objectivity of being and the objective truth of science became really a problem for him. The naive objectivity of common sense and science, divorced from the concrete subjectivity that performs and generates, could no longer be accepted. The real problem for Hume accordingly lay in the "world-riddle" (as Husserl puts it) in the deeper and ultimate sense. And put in phenomenological terms, the latter would finally mean the riddle of a world whose very being is one constituted through "subjective achievement" *(Sein aus subjektiver Leistung)*.[15]

However, with all its fictionalism, Husserl observes, Humean positivism hardly goes beyond a psychological theory of knowledge, i.e., an explanation of knowledge on the basis of empirical-psychological analysis. As such, it never did amount to a theory of knowledge in the specific transcendental-philosophical sense.[16] It was left only to the philosophy of Kant to take up the positive cue contained in Humeanism and to make out of it a constructive philosophy in the shape of "transcendental subjectivism". Husserl's use of the key expression "transcendental" should be clarified in this context. It serves as the leading concept in the Husserlian problem of tracing back – indeed as Husserl puts it, "questioning back" *(Rückfrage)* – the final source of all forms of knowing; it thus entails the reflection of knowing on its own subjectivity, in which all knowledge-validating forms originate. This supposed source, on further analysis, is denoted as "I-self" *(Ich-selbst)*, with the totality of its actual and possible life of knowing. To anticipate the transcendental problem in phenomenology, it moves around the relation of this "I" to "my" mind and to my life in the world, of which I am conscious and whose true being I recognise in my own knowledge-forms *(Erkenntnisgebilden)*.

[14] The reference here is again to the Husserlian critique of science in general, q.v. Chap. VII.

[15] *Krisis*, 25, p. 100.

[16] Cf. Husserl, Manuscript M I 1: "Phänomenologie und Erkenntnistheorie", III. 5–6.

IV

Husserl's attitude towards the nineteenth century "empirio-critical positivism" of Germany is also worth considering in this connection. The German positivists, like Mach and Avenarius, had introduced the "empirio-critical" method and theory of knowledge as against the prevailing transcendental-idealist philosophy of their time, by reducing truth to sense-contents. Further they rejected that there is essentially an opposition between the inner world of the subject and the outer world, and advocated the ideal of strict scientificity. Moreover, the positivist theory of "the economy of thought" – *Denkökonomie* – sought to interpret theoretical and scientific processes of man directly on the analogy of technical practice and its resulting economy. Accordingly, laws of thought are simply explained as instruments of the so-called economy of thinking, i.e., economically ordered experience lying ready for use.

In his assessment of the empirio-critical positivism – particularly that of Mach – Husserl discovers the signs of phenomenological thinking already present. The phenomenological method of acquiring knowledge through the pure description of the given alone, and also the aim of establishing philosophy as a "strict science", as adopted by Husserl, largely reflect the background of empirio-critical positivism. However, when Husserl attempted a phenomenological reorientation of pure logic and theory of knowledge *("Neubegründung der reinen Logik und Erkenntnistheorie")*, he expressly departed from empirio-criticism. Regarding the description of the given, Husserl obviously does not think of the sensuously perceptible givenness, but of one which we obtain through another way of comprehending, viz., eidetic or intuitional comprehension of essences or essential structures of consciousness.

Husserl further opposes the positivist theory of *"Denkökonomie"*. At first approving of Mach's analysis of the economy of scientific practice in knowing *(Erkenntnispraxis)*, Husserl warns against the epistemological consequences which Mach had drawn out of these analyses. For Mach, laws are nothing but sort of technical instruments for the economic ordering of the multiplicity of empirical data. Husserl, on the other hand, takes this principle of unification as implied by *"Denkökonomie"* as partaking of an anthropological-psychological character. The *a priori* validity of mathematical and logical categories and principles should, according to Husserl, be looked upon as the presupposition of the significant teachings of *Denkökonomie* rather than its result. Consequently, Husserl argues against this theory almost in the same way as against psychologism. Just as psychologism mistakenly explains the ideal character of logical reasoning as the result of a psychical act, so also *Denkökonomie* seeks to trace the logical-ideal conditions of thought in its analysis of the so-called "economic" nature of theoretical experimenting. (On this point Husserl would rather agree with Neo-Kantianism as against psychologism and *Denkökonomie*).

With all his criticism of *Denkökonomie*, Husserl at the same time accepted Mach as one who had prepared the way to phenomenological method through his analysis of sensations. Husserl would even go furter to characterise the positivistic empiricism of Avenarius and Schuppe as a form of "transcendental philosophy".[17]

V

As already stated, the philosophy of Kant serves for Husserl as the model of a truly transcendental philosophy; indeed the former shows for Husserl the concrete possibility for a system of "philosophy as strict science" – *"Philosophie als strenge Wissenschaft"*, the motto adopted by Husserl for the programme of his phenomenological philosophy at quite an early stage. And this could be possible with Kantianism, because it had posited an original source, out of which the categorial forms of knowledge originate and through which they are validated, – the source in subjectivity. The Kantian philosophy is one which proposes to return to the knowing subjectivity as the source through which all meanings of objectivity are formed and validated. Thus in its critique of experience it undertakes to interpret the world of objectivity in terms of meaning forms and modes of validaton; and all these ultimately lead to a new kind of scientific standard in philosophy.

[17] *Die Krisis*, § 56.

So, leaving aside Humean scepticism, the Kantian system for the first time attempts a universal transcendental philosophy, meant as strict science. Husserl himself seeks to develop this very idea of philosophy as a transcendental science in the shape of phenomenology as a 'science of pure consciousness'. Here it may be asked why Hume's scepticism, though containing subjective psychology and being subjective in method, still falls far short of such a science of consciousness as envisaged in phenomenology. The emphasis in Humeanism is, of course, shifted from the world of objectivity to the sphere of consciousness. But in such transference the method that is adopted is a psychological one – that of reducing in terms of "impressions".

Reduction, although in a different sense, is also the method of phenomenology. Indeed the method of transcendental reduction is the fundamental method of phenomenology and its approach to the thematic domain of philosophy, i.e., transcendental subjectivity, according to phenomenology. Phenomenological reduction indicates the switching over from the naturalist standpoint to a new one, which may serve as the avenue to the whole field of absolute consciousness. The motto of phenomenological reduction is to trace back "to the things themselves" – "*zu den Sachen selbst*", as the Husserlian slogan puts it. The "things" here referred to are, of course, not the real objects or facts, but rather the immediately evident "phenomena" within the region of *purified* experience. "Phenomena" in the phenomenological sense are those that just appear to the reflecting consciousness as the self-given *essences* of the objects of experience.

Now the empiricist program of reduction, as in Humeanism, seems apparently similar to the phenomenological procedure, so far as in the former there is the movement from objective categories back to the impressions themselves. Indeed, generally speaking, in both the concern is rather for the way in which our knowledge of object is gained than on the object as such. Moreover, the two systems seem to share in broad the negative aspect of the program – namely, freedom from presuppositions and beliefs. The "negative result" of phenomenology in respect of metaphysical knowledge of Being can well be compared to the sceptical position of Hume. And in phenomenology – somewhat as in Hume – the method of reduction prevents rash metaphysical hypostasization.[18]

But the difference between the two methods of reduction is only too evident, as already pointed out. In a word, the empiricist reduction is marked by the bias of over-simplification in terms of sense-data alone, missing altogether the possible role of a deeper essentialistic insight. The apparent similarity in respect of the said negative aspect also should not be overemphasized. Phenomenology seeks to go further than the aim of merely removing the theoretical preconceptions in order to get back to the immediate data of consciousness. The whole world of natural experience, and all theories and sciences which relate to this world, are subjected to radical suspension or "bracketing". On the implication of phenomenological reduction, Fink, a close critic of Phenomenology, observes: "To eliminate the worldly belief in the depth of its transcendental origin is to perform the phenomenological reduction".[19]

Closely related to reduction is the concept of *analysis*, occurring in common in the philosophies of positivism and phenomenology alike – particularly in view of the role of analysis in modern logical positivist philosophy. Now, so far as the phenomenological principle of analysis is concerned, it is essentially contained in tracing back from the given complex of experience to the simple elements of "phenomena". To clarify the import of the latter, it consists of the meaning of object *(Gegenstandssinn)* as it stands through the neutralising of the factual character of the object.[20] From this it follows that a systematic phenomenology would not direct its efforts towards a real analysis of experience. For, the immanent study of pure experience, the study of the genuine essences evident therein, should not be mistaken for a study of the real components of experience.

Under the naturalistic motive of psychology such a mistake is apt to be committed. And such is the case with the sensualisitic analysis of experience in the Humean system. Impressions and ideas in the latter are looked upon as real components of ex-

[18] See L. Landgrebe, "Phenomenology and Metaphysics", *Philosophy and Phenomenological Research*, Dec. 1949.

[19] Eugen Fink, "Die phänomenologische Philosophie in der gegenwärtigen Kritik", *Kant-Studien*, Bd. 38 (1933).

[20] Cf. E. Fink, "Operative Begriffe in Husserls Phänomenologie", *Zeitschrift für philosophische Forschung*, Bd. XI, p. 321ff., 1957.

perience, and only as passive elements devoid of any intentional referentiality. The whole direction of psychologistic atomism from the sense-given to the corresponding simple elements has missed the double correspondence between the bipolar aspects of the intentional act, viz., the "noematic" and the "noetic" correlates. This bipolarity of "noema" and "noesis" – the former referring to the terminus in intentional consciousness, and the latter meaning the apprehension itself as directed upon the noema – forms one of the central concerns in the phenomenological enquiry.

VI

Analysis has been carried in a widely different direction by the modern Positivists and is to be sharply distinguished from the phenomenological type of analysis. Analytical or logical positivism, in common with the positivism or empiricism of the original type, seeks to interpret the world in terms of sense data or sense contents. But the approach is chiefly through the logical analysis of language, i.e., through forms of propositions which state our knowledge of the world. The task of philosophy accordingly would lie not in the discovery of any new kind of facts but in the clarification of propositions and their relations in language. Thus positivistic analysis – particularly the linguistic analysis in "ordinary language philosophy" – is concerned with the finding of equivalent expressions, but with simpler structure.[21]

The logical positivist program of analysis is thus concerned only with the logical structure of language rather than with the meant content. The phenomenological analysis, on the other hand, is not as such concerned with linguistic expressions, but rather with the "phenomena" within the region of immanent experience – and linguistic symbols may serve only as external index to such phenomena. Here the task of analysis is to trace the elements and structure obtained through phenomenological reduction and intuition.

---

[21] Cf. "By analysis they (the analytical philosophers) meant something which whatever precise description of it they chose, at least involved the attempt to rewrite in different and in some way more appropriate terms those statements which they found philosophically puzzling." J. O. Urmson, *Philosophical Analysis*, p. vii.

Of course, even for the phenomenologist, certain verbal expressions may and do provide the point of departure for analysis; but that would only be to unfold the meaning implicated in the form of phenomena meant. In "Logical Investigations", for instance, Husserl raises the question of the phenomenological and intentional differentiation in expressions, having the physical and the psychical side of meaning.[22] With regard to names, he points to a distinction between what they "demonstrate" and what they signify, and sometimes to a distinction between that which a name signifies – its meaning or the content of nominal representation – and that which it names, i.e., the object of that representation.

In his analysis of meaning, Husserl further draws a distinction between what he calls "occasional" and "objective" expressions – particularly in view of such expressions that have reference to the momentary content of demonstration, and as such belong to a further stage of expressions, whose meanings change from case to case.[23] The meaning of the former type of expressions is dependent upon the context of the speaking person, while that of the latter is not so dependent but rather fixed in its apparent content. An objective expression is to be understood without reference to the context of the person speaking and to the circumstances under which his expressions occurs. On the other hand, an expression that is essentially subjective or occasional is one to which a conceptually united group of possible meanings so belong that it is essential for the expressions concerned to orientate its actual meaning according to the speaking person and his position.[24]

The point of reference for the logical positivist is, after all, the elementary facts and factual relations, corresponding to which stand the simple elementary propositions – "atomic propositions", as Russell and Wittgenstein, for example, would hold. The unit of analysis is in any case the elementary propositions – or

---

[22] *Logische Untersuchungen*, Vol. II, I. i. 6.

[23] *Ibid.*, I. vii. 26.

[24] Although *Log. Untersuchungen* (vol. II) is largely preoccupied with the question of the meaning of words, phenomenology cannot, strictly speaking, be branded as a "theory of meaning" (Bedeutungslehre). Those investigations in connection with meaning serve rather as preparation for a fuller epistemological explanation, and nothing further. Cf. "Entwurf einer Vorrede zu den Logischen Untersuchungen" (1913), § 10, ed. by E. Fink in *Tijdschrift voor Philosophie*, 1939.

"protocol sentences", as certain positivists like Neurath would posit. In the case of logical atomism, approaching the immediately sense-given in terms of simple sentence, some sort of linguistic solipsism may seem almost to be inevitable. But that would be far from a possibility, so far as the very nature of phenomenological analysis is concerned.

The difference between the analyst's doctrine of linguistic use and the phenomenological analysis in terms of intentionality need not, however, be over-emphasized. For, so far as ordinary language philosophy in particular is concerned, its peculiar reference to "grammar" takes into view "what it makes sense to say". And thereby it seems to come closer to the phenomenological approach to the eidetic meaning structures of what are present to reflection. For both, the world is accepted to be "familiar" (an expression typical for analytical philosophy – more or less corresponding to the "naturalistic attitude" in phenomenological philosophy). For both, again, the socalled familiarit is as much a problem to be dealt with through adequate methodology.

In this connection it may be noted that Wittgenstein, in his later development (in *Philosophische Untersuchungen*) seems to come strangely close to the fundamental attitude of the phenomenological method of intuiting. His motto has thus been "not to think but to look".[25] According to Wittgenstein, philosophy lays bare the uses of language; it seeks no more than to exhibit the actual functioning of language. In all his explanation of language, Wittgenstein's general aim is to break the rigidity of the terms used in our thought. He does not even offer any thesis or doctrine of his own. He rather claims to describe the various workings of language and to lay them before us. He attempts to proceed in terms of what "goes on" in our experience, and not by merely studying the grammatical structures of the expressions used to mean the contents of consciousness concerned.

Logical positivism means to attribute to philosophy a region of logical consequences and precision, worked out scientifically in order to eliminate thereby the unclarities and contradictions. And apparently a similar task of winning for philosophy its own domain of strictly scientific investigations is no doubt undertaken

---

[25] *Philosophical Investigations* I. 66.

in another way by Husserl also. But in pursuing this goal, the latter went from the actuality of facts to the ideality of essences and to their systematic description; positivism, on the other hand, chose rather the opposite way of referring back from concepts to facts, and took accordingly the logical analysis of language as the only domain of philosophy. In a word, the linguistic analysis of the positivist is committed to the world of facts, whereas phenomenological analysis proposes to be free exactly from such commitment. Moreover, while the positivist analyses language as the passive and formal vehicle of factual reference, the phenomenologist analyses the double aspect of the intentional act of consciousness – the noetic, i.e., act-wise and the noematic, i.e., content-wise.

In a sense both positivism and phenomenology would agree negatively that philosophy should not include "matters of fact" within its proper domain. Thus Hume admitted that he was concerned philosophically not with "matters of fact" but with "relations of ideas", which are only immanent in thought. And Husserl expressly "brackets" the natural world of facts, and discovers transcendental (non-mental) essences within the immanent region of pure consciousness. In this sense both would turn to subjectivism.[26] But while with Hume subjectivity is only another name for fictionality and is just a nominal term for the atomistic mental states, for Husserl subjectivity is an autonomous region of *ideal* contents having transcendental status. The Humean tradition of fictionalism shows itself in modern positivism also, in the form of bare linguistic structure of propositions – leaving, again, no scope for an autonomous region like the supposed one of "pure consciousness".

VII

This brings us to the two fundamentally different attitudes towards the notion of subjectivity as in Humean positivism in particular and in Husserlian phenomenology. The Humean definition of subjectivity may be characterized simply as natural-

---

[26] The specific question of subjectivism in phenomenology and its notion of subjectivity have been treated in a subsequent chapter of the book (Ch. IV).

psychological. Subjectivity is just taken to be equivalent to mentality (i.e., to be mental); and what is mind other than a composite bundle of fleeting atomic perceptions? As such subjectivity has no *locus standi* apart from the discrete mental states bound together through association. To Husserl, on the other hand, subjectivity is a fundamental truth – the subjectivity of the pure ego. This subjectivity, however, should not in any case be taken in the narrower sense of empirical-psychological subjectivity. The phenomenological concern with "transcendental subjectivity" does not imply in any way a return to an introspectionistic subjective psychology – whether in point of methodology or of the resulting doctrine. (We leave the topic to be discussed subsequently – see Ch. IV).

As for the concept of ego, Husserl speaks of subjectivity generally in the context of the ego, the identical subject pole of several acts of consciousness. In his earlier phase (1st edition of *Logische Untersuchungen*, Book II), however, Husserl had rejected the notion of an identical subject as the necessary centre of reference beyond the intentional acts of consciousness, and sided rather with the Humean trend of "empirical I". But subsequently (already in the 2nd edition of the same[27]) he shifted from the empiricist position, and gradually came to recognise an integral status of the ego. In *Ideen* I, he posited the indubitable reality of the ego (in a Cartesian way) in relation to the contingent world.[28]

Now, apart from the atomistic tradition, in contemporary analytical philosophy (as conspicuously in Ryle's *The Concept of Mind*) a thoroughly empirical-analytical neo-behaviouristic theory of mind and ego has been attempted. As a result of the positivistic concept of mind as nothing more than "minding", a notion of "I" as merely an index term is sought to substitute the concept of I-self of the Cartesian tradition. But what the positivist, in the name of objective analysis, resolves in linguistic-behaviouristic terms, appears to be a fundamental concrete datum for the phenomenologist with his inner-subjective attitude. Every conscious act pertains to the act-performing Ego, being directed from it. The pure Ego not only serves as the centre of all

---

[27] *Log. Untersuchungen*, Vol. II (2nd edition), V. i. 8 (Zusatz).
[28] As regards the position of Ego in a phenomenological view of consciousness, and the problem in that connection, see *infra*, Ch. V – particularly, sec. 7.

reference, but it also proves to be the irremovable principle, the residuum, through all possible phenomenological disconnections.

However, it may be pointed out in this connection that even in Husserl's phenomenology, we find an approach through the analysis of the expression "I".[29] Husserl makes it clear that the word "I", as a personal pronoun, lacks the objective character which is otherwise conveyed by those expressions that are called by him "objective" (q.v. sec. 6 of this chapter). For it is a word with which the speaker marks himself. Each speaking person has his I-representation *(Ichvorstellung)*, and therewith his individual conception of I; therefore, for each person the meaning of the word is different. Yet so far as each person, in speaking of himself, uses the word "I", the latter possesses the universal mark referring to this fact. But the word "I" has not in itself the capacity directly to arouse the particular I-representation which determines the concrete meaning in the context of the speech concerned. It rather possesses an *indicating* function of addressing, as it were, to the hearer: "the person over against you is meaning himself". Thus, for Husserl, the linguistic approach to the meaning of I should be looked only as an indicating step, hinting at some deeper essence behind the word itself. And he further anticipates the danger of accepting the immediate representation of the speaking person as the comprehension of the complete meaning of the term "I" in its own essence.

The typical phenomenological investigation into the "constitution" of the individual human ego – what Husserl calls "I-man" *(Ich-Mensch)* – may throw some further light in this direction – as we shall see subsequently (q. v. Ch. V). The analysis undertaken in that connection would not confine itself to the bare empirical physico-mental I, having body and mind; it would further lead to a "pure mental I" *(rein seelisches Ich)*. Here lies the sharp difference between the empirical-positivist and the phenomenological way of approach. The pure ego is to be understood essentially as the *subject* of acts and states directing itself through the acts to the objects. And both aspects of pure I in relation to its functionality are to be recognised – namely, one as distinguished from the acts and another as inseparably

---

[29] Vide *Log. Untersuchungen,* Vol. I, II. iii. 26.

related to them. Indeed Husserl speaks of a peculiar transcendence – "a transcendence in immanence" – in respect of the so-called pure Ego.[30] And this element of transcendence is the deciding factor which makes possible the phenomenological recognition of the pure Ego in sharp distinction from the empirical ego (the only ego recognised in empirical philosophy).

Indeed behind all his assertions concerning over-empirical subject and subjectivity, Husserl counts on a deeper insight than the merely psychological one, and thus finds in it an approach to a pure field of experience – that of "transcendental subjectivity". Guided neither by nominalism nor by conceptualism, Husserl sought to follow a new, and enriched, form of intuitionism – one that promises a system of critique of experience.

[30] Vide *Ideen* I, § 57.

CHAPTER III

HUSSERL'S CRITIQUE OF FORMAL LOGIC[1]

I

The role of logic taken in a strict sense within the philosophical discipline at large has not always been an undisputed problem with philosophers. Even though pure formal logic had been recognized – and hardly could it be overlooked – its place has been variously indicated. Thus, in certain theories, logic has been taken as philosophically comprehensive; Leibniz, for example, went in for "mathesis universalis" as yielding a complete and automatic language of reasoning. At other place – for instance, in Aristotle – logic would provide one philosophical discipline among others. And sometimes again, it is conceived as having a very restricted field of operation, namely, as the theory of demonstration without any further bearing on philosophical thought (as in Hume). Modern logic, again, with its mathematically oriented generalized apparatus of thought, claims to go further than traditional logic, so far as – at least with a substantial section of contemporary philosophers – "it is the method of philosophizing itself", as Carnap states it.

Of all these orientations of logic in the philosophical discipline at large, it is perhaps in Hume's theory alone that a critique of logical principles from a philosophical point of view could be found to be present. But a pronounced and sharper critique of logic can be met with in the phenomenology of Husserl in his attempt at formulating a genuinely "philosophical logic" – one that might overcome the limitations and shortcomings of tradi-

---

[1] This discourse has chiefly been based on two major works of Husserl, viz., *Formale und transzendentale Logik* (Halle, Niemeyer, 1929) and *Erfahrung und Urteil, Untersuchungen zur Genealogie der Logik* (Hamburg, 1948).

tional formal logic. Husserl, however, never did deny logic as the science of pure forms. Indeed he recognized the theory of forms of judgment as the primary formal-logical discipline. But that hardly means that such a discipline should provide the method of philosophizing – be it in the rationalist (Leibnizian) or in the positivist manner. On the contrary, Husserl presents the case for a "higher" logic which should provide the fundamental criticism of the forms of traditional logic. In other words, what Husserl seems to be interested in may rightly be called "meta-logic" rather than logic as such.[2]

However, in characterizing the Husserlian treatment of logic as "meta-logic", we need not at once take Husserl's philosophical logic to be affiliated to the "metalogic" that results from the logistics of Lukasiewicz and Tarski. The latter proposed to formalise logical system, analogous to the "meta-mathematics" of Hilbert. Nor is the phenomenological treatment of logic to be regarded as metalogic in Carnap's sense of "statements about statements and parts of statements" obtained through the logical analysis of language. That his logical deliberations in a sense amount to statements about statements, i.e., meta-statements, Husserl might agree – and even perhaps like Carnap, that they are in the given language itself. But as to the exact way of deriving such statements, Husserl would offer an entirely different explanation. In proposing logic as "theory of science" *(Wissenschaftslehre)*, Husserl indeed subscribes to the attitude of the critical subject who "does not plainly judge but judges over judgment".

Now, what Husserl proposes is a "philosophical logic" which should not only bring out the foundations and rationale of traditional logic, but should at the same time provide the genuine method of philosophizing itself. However, such philosophical logic is not meant in the *metaphysical* sense of idealist logic, be it Hegelian or Bradleyan. Nor, on the other hand, would it coincide with the other end of logical discipline, viz., analytical logic, also termed "philosophical logic" by Bertrand Russell, meaning that discipline which is to render the knowledge of logical forms involved in all understanding of discourse, explicit and pure.[3] The

---

[2] Cf. J. N. Mohanty, *Husserl's Theory of Meaning*, Ch. VI; the expression "meta-logic" has been used to indicate Husserl's treatment of logic in broad.

[3] Cf. B. Russell, "Logic as the Essence of Philosophy" in *Our Knowledge of the External world*.

latter type of logic proceeds through *abstraction* from the concrete
contents, unlike in the Husserlian logic.

II

Husserl indeed recognizes logic as the "science of pure forms";
there is no question of his denying it in the strict narrow sense.
He refers to the pure theory of forms of judgment as "the first
formal-logical discipline". To start with, formal logic stands as
"apophantic analytic", so far as it is concerned with the problem
of formalization in the apophantic sphere, i.e., with respect to
assertive statements or judgments in the strict sense. But on
Husserl's view, the logic started by Aristotle was hardly able to
work out in full freedom the scope of term-variables and the
purity of the idea of "form". For Aristotle's Analytic does contain
reference to the real world, and as such does not exclude from
its scope the concept of *reality*. In this respect Husserl would
admit the excellence of modern mathematical logic, wherein
the introduction of algebra makes room for a pure formal logic.[4]

The idea of the theory of forms concerns the bare possibility
of judgments *qua* judgments, irrespective of whether they are
true or false. The question whether judgments as judgments are
consistent or contradictory should alone be relevant in the
classification of judgments in accordance with *form*. Now, a form
of judgment has to be considered in relation to a universal type,
under which not only all possible determinate judgments of that
form can be brought, but also all pure forms subordinated to the
original form. For instance, if the form "S is P" is taken as a
universal type, the form "Sp is q" may be subordinated to it;
and to the latter again the form "(Sp) q is r" can be similarly
subordinated. The latter two forms illustrate a multiplicity of
possible forms as "modifications" of the universal type. This
brings us to the original form *(Urform)* that determines the sub-
ordinate forms – in this case, the form of the judgment "S is p".

Indeed, going a step further, Husserl recognizes the concept

---

[4] In his earliest work, *Philosophie der Arithmetik*, Husserl referred to the function of
symbols as the apparatus of intellect in serving the economy of mental performance
("Ökonomie der geistigen Arbeitsleistung") just as instruments and machines serve the
economy of mechanical performance.

of "operation" as the guiding factor in our investigation of forms. The fundamental operations and their laws, as well as the ideal construction of the infinity of forms, have to be demonstrated. The universal forms of construction as the conjunctive and the hypothetical indicate the fundamental forms of operation. This concept indeed seems to come close to the concept of "function" or rather "truth-function" in modern logic, in so far as in the latter the truth-value of the compounded or negated proposition is determined by the truth-value of its original expressions.

III

Within formal logic itself Husserl introduces a subtle distinction between the logic of non-contradiction and the logic of truth – a distinction which he himself claims to be a novel one. What he calls the "logic of consistency" or "logic of non-contradiction" emerges as the second step in formal logic out of the primary stage of "formal apophansis". As the science of the possible forms of true judgment. the former concerns the conditions of possible truth and falsity for all conceivable judgments. Accordingly the logic of consistency or of non-contradiction has to find out the essential laws governing the analytic agreement and disagreement of judgments – their analytic non-contradiction; the question about the truth and falsity of propositions should not arrive at this stage of formal logic.

Syllogistic and mathematical analysis belong to the level of a pure apophantic analytic. In the context of the latter Husserl would come close, at least in principle, to the formalism in Hilbert's philosophy of mathematics, when the latter argues that the consistency of a postulate system may be established without the production of a model. But Husserl takes a different turn from a purely *formalistic* definition of non-contradiction; he would rather define the latter as the possibility on the part of the judging agent to judge in all clearness within the unity of a judgment. And the dual principles of contradiction and excluded middle correspond in the logic of consistency to a principle that belongs to the essence of judgments proper, i.e., to those which are themselves given in the evidence of clearness. Thus, two contradictory judgments, both of which can equally be brought to the evidence of clearness, cannot be possible at the same time. The scope of the principle of non-contradiction is further extended when it is shown to comprehend not merely the possible but also the *compossible* forms of true judgment. "Compossibility" only indicates the joining of judgments to the unity of a collective judgment.

Although non-contradiction as such may constitute an essential condition of possible truth, it hardly amounts to a formal logic of truth in the strict sense. But Husserl would go further to show that the transition from the logic of consistency (which he also calls "pure analytic") to that of truth is not hard to gain; on the contrary, it is a transition which is necessary. Now truth and falsity are predicates which can only belong to a *clear* judgment actually drawn. And pure analytical logic, i.e., logic of pure consistency, is concerned with the region of the essential type of clear judgments. Thus viewed, a pure analytic is at the same time a real part of the formal logic of truth. For, each pure consistency of judgment, when performed in the light of "intuition" *(Anschauung)*, turns into a consistency of truth or of actual possibility. Though non-contradiction is an essential condition for the possibility of truth, the bare analytic transforms itself into a formal logic of truth.

In approaching the problem in this manner, Husserl admittedly departs from the traditional way of distinguishing these two logics. The traditional distinction between non-contradiction and truth had been generally interpreted otherwise. On the one hand, there is the formal-logical problematic in general, wherefrom all "matters of knowledge" would as such be excluded; on the other hand, there would arise the problems of logic in some wider sense, taking into account the factual contents as well as the questions of the possibility of knowledge of reality. Husserl's classification in this regard – one that he himself claims indeed to be a novel one – would largely correspond to the distinction respectively between "implication" and inference in modern logic, rather than between formal logic and material logic. As with the concept of "implication", the logic of consistency deals only with the question of pure logical derivation rather than with the truth of the conclusion. The logic of truth, on the contrary, being as much *formal*, stands for more than mere implication and extends to the level of truth-assertion. And as Stebbing clearly points out, the difference is there as between "*asserting* a proposition and merely *considering* or *contemplating* or *assuming* it".[5]

IV

Towards traditional formal logic, conceived as "apophantic analytic", Husserl assumes a critical attitude. Traditional formal logic would appear to suffer from an inevitable limitation, if we look for a logic in general, a "theory of science" *(Wissenschafts-lehre)*, in such logic. What Husserl means by this is a logic which should indeed be formal – but "in a new richer sense". The failure of traditional logic to meet this demand is attributed to the conceptual seclusion of traditional logic, arising from the Aristotelian concept of judgmental form. This concept can be understood also as the determination of judgments in general exclusively through their "syntactical forms", and formal logic *a priori* represents the latter as forms of syntactical operation.

But this restricted notion of the "formal" affects, Husserl points out, "the radical purity" of formal logic; and it is this purity alone that can make formal logic philosophically useful and even important to the highest extent. Husserl rightly points out – as did modern mathematical logic – that the Aristotelian use of variables, within the framework of fundamental apophantic forms and their derivatives, largely misses the scope of a truly generalized logic.

This awareness of the "conceptual seclusion" of traditional logic takes Husserl further to suggest the idea of an enlarged analytic, wherein a synthesis of the traditional syllogistic and the formal-mathematical analysis would find place. And the primary model for such an integration of syllogistic within the framework of formal mathematics could be found in the Leibnizan idea of "mathesis universalis". The latter arose, Husserl recognizes, out of the need of deductive technique in mathematical science rather than from an internal necessity of the system itself.[6]

<hr>

[5] L. S. Stebbing, *A Modern Introduction to Logic*, p. 212.
[6] Definite steps in this direction towards formulating a logical calculus, on the model of algebra, were taken later by Boole, de Morgan and others.

This unity of logic and mathematics had two consequences. On the one hand, syllogistic had to undergo a changed interpretation within the scope of a comprehensive logic *(Umfangslogik)*. But on the other hand, new logic did retain the "intellectual core" in continuity with the traditional analytic. And by this Husserl evidently means the essentially *formal* character of the generalized logic as much as of the Aristotelian Analytic.

The unification of logic with mathematics, however, leads to a new region, viz., that of "Formal Ontology". From Aristotelian analytic would follow a formal apophantic mathematics, pertaining to predication. Now, formal mathematical disciplines, including the theory of numbers, are *formal* in the sense that they have as fundamental concepts certain forms of derivation pertaining to something in general. Accordingly the whole of mathematics can be understood in the light of an *a priori* theory of objects. In other words, an ontology, though a *formal* one, would come into play as related to the pure modes of something.[7]

Husserl further explains the transition from formal apophantic logic to formal ontology. Formal logic proceeds consistently on the path of seeking formal conditions of possible truth; and the logical science derives its form from the structure of propositions. Thus by virtue of the meaning lying in propositions themselves, the science of logic is led to objectivities. In judging we primarily refer to objects; and the objective has its possible categorial forms – forms of the type of modes of *something-in-general*. The character of "form" arises at the level of categorially determined judgments – not as real psychical datum but as intentional correlates of positing. But that is a theme relating to the origin of the logical form, which we consider subsequently (Section 7).

The analytic, as the formal theory of science, is thus transposed into formal ontology, so far as the former is objectively directed, or "ontically directed", as Husserl would put it. The theme of analytic logic is constituted by categorial objectivities in general according to their pure forms. Consequently, analytic logic can even be characterized as *ontological* by virtue of its *a priori* gener-

---

[7] Although the idea of a "formal ontology" was already introduced in Husserl's earlier work, *Logische Untersuchungen*, the close relation between the formal-ontological *a priori* and the apophantic *a priori* was discussed only later in *Formale und transzendentale Logik*.

ality. And that is what is meant by the Husserlian concept of "Formal ontology".

This introduction of formal ontology, however, should not be interpreted as an attempt, on Husserl's part, of ontologizing on the basis of formal logic. For Husserl draws a sharp distinction between the two attitudes – one apophantic and the other ontological. To view judgments thematically in their syntactical unity is one thing, and to direct out attention to objects and their constituting forms is another. The recognition of the empty form of region in general in the ontological attitude does not stand in the way of the formal-analytic character of logic.

Thus, what Husserl prefers to call "philosophical logic" has to relate itself, unlike formal mathematics and logic, to the question of *application* – indefinite, ideally possible application of the formal-logical meaning. It does not approve of a mathematics which is altogether free from the idea of possible application. Rather the task of philosophical logic should be to see that formal mathematics is originally logical analytic, but is extended in knowledge-function through intentionality in knowing.

V

So with regard to formal logic Husserl takes up a two-fold position. On the one hand, Husserl does not mean to deny formal logic at all; on the contrary, he is in favour of obtaining one on a more generalized level. But at the same time he recognizes a new region of investigation that emerges from mathematics, viz., formal ontology. Formal logic and mathematics would then provide the point of departure for an *a priori* theory of object or ontology – although, as already indicated, formal apophantic and formal ontology represent *one* logic, only treated in two attitudes.

Now, categorially formed objectivity is admittedly no apophantic concept, but an ontological one. Shifting from the attitude of apophantic logic which deals with judgments as apophantic meanings, Husserl refers to the attitude of formal-ontological logic towards possible categorial objectivities themselves and their forms. But in recognizing the status of the forms of categorial objectivities themselves, as beyond mere meaning-forms in judgment, Husserl evidently admits the transcendence of thought from its immanent syntactical forms in judging to some objectivities, although not those of factual natural science. And a non-empiricist as Husserl admittedly is, the apriority pertaining to the forms of thought are not sought to be reduced in terms of sense-presentations.

At this stage the issue that comes out is: how does the Husserlian position regarding forms of thought confront with the formalist thesis? Formalists abide by the definition of "form" as an invariant structure independent of special matter, and the key to formalistic reduction is by way of syntactic-semantic forms of statements. If any necessity be recognized by formalists, it should exclusively belong to the non-sensible relations or patterns within the framework of statements themselves. So to be consistent with the formalist positions, all transcendences have to be left out as logically meangless. For neither would categorical objectivities imply tautologies, nor does judging about them include empirical statements, such as Carnap would mean when he refers to the so-called "protocol statements".

As Wittgenstein has proposed, the formalist way of interpreting philosophical propositions would be to cover the whole field of significant discourse by formal statements on the one hand and empirical statements on the other. Carnap, again, described the structure of language by assigning the various types of linguistic expressions or concepts their respective places in a deductive hierarchy which should belong to the realm of formal truths. He carried the formalist program further through the logical syntax of the language of science. Stressing exclusively on the rules of formation and transformation, Carnap sought to dispense with meaning-rules which could correlate linguistic expressions with observable states of affair.

Now in an exclusively semantic approach to philosophy, insisting on formal techniques, the element of experience would evidently present itself as a factor hardly to be resolved formalistically. The attempt to interpret *all* philosophical statements as syntactical may, on ultimate analysis, prove to be baffling even for a positivist. And this would hold good particularly for what Carnap classifies as "experience-expressions", which, as Ayer critically points out, need not be regarded as syntactical terms.[8] The question as to what should count as an *experience* becomes important. An arbitrary decision in this regard can hardly settle the question.

Again, the positivist principle of verifiability, even though taken in a "weaker" sense, demands that a statement should be capable of being in some degree confirmed or disconfirmed by observation. Unless the statement concerned is itself an elementary statement, it had to be such that elementary statements could support it; but they need not necessarily *entail* it or its negation. As Ayer again points out, this notion of "confirmation" has never yet been adequately formalized. Perhaps it cannot be – so long as the structure of experience is sought to be resolved entirely with reference to the syntactical forms of language, and to them alone.

Loosely in Aristotelian apophantic logic and rigorously in modern mathematical logic, all thought is thus sought to be formalized through the equation of the forms of thought with the syntactical forms of statement. Consequently, whatever in thought is not so amenable to formalization is rejected, and as a result all the drastic elimination of all transcendences would follow. A modified solution – a seeming compromise – in this problem of relating form and content has, however, been suggested by Ryle in the shape of what he choses to call "informal logic".[9] *Prima facie* he admits that all philosophical concepts are not open to formalization; for while formal logic operates with "topic-neutral" expressions which are the logical constants, philosophy has to do with the topical or subject-matter concepts. The typical themes of the philosopher, such as pleasure, colour, the future etc., (to cite Ryle's own examples) can hardly be treated as topic-neutral, and consequently cannot be formalized. Even the topic-neutral expressions, with which formal logic is to deal, hold good within a restricted field.

The formalistic strain, however, shows itself perhaps in a feeble way, when Ryle goes on to say that both formal logic as well as philosophical discourse broadly share in common what is

[8] Cf. Ayer, Introduction in *Logical Positivism*: ". . . 'experience-expression' is not a syntactical term".
[9] Vide G. Ryle, *Dilemmas*, VIII.

usually denoted, in a neutral way, as "logical considerations". Thus the best approximation that Ryle can suggest towards a formalization of philosophical discourse is by way of investigating the *special content* of the subject-matter concepts as well as their logical behaviour. Formal logic, on the other hand, should be concerned with determining "exchange-equivalents" (i.e., equivalents in terms of experience) of the logical constants, although with the help of the calculus of constants within the framework of a deductive system.

Now, Ryle's prescription of the analysis of special content and the observation of the logical behaviour of philosophical concepts seems to throw no further light ont he form-content problem. For the question would remain: how far does the special content determine the logical form – as admittedly there is one – of the topical concept? But the so-called "special content" does seem to contribute to the typical *aformal* character of the concepts; otherwise they would stand on the same footing as topic-neutral expressions. In that case, again, the so-called "logical behaviour" should rather be sought for in the special content itself, granting that the latter reveals some inner structure within itself.

VI

This brings us to the more general question regarding the possibility of *synthetic a priori*. So far as the sphere of pure formal logic is concerned, Husserl would not advocate apriority beyond the *analytical* – and that confines it practically to the sphere of formal tautologies. But when Husserl comes to the idea of a universal *a priori* "theory of science", he finds the necessity of supplementing the analytical-formal by a "material" theory of science. In determining the concept of "analytic *a priori*" through pure formal analytic, the idea of a new "synthetic *a priori*" comes into question – the idea of such material and universal *a priori* as might connect together all material *a priori* regions in a totality. And this prompts Husserl to draw a fundamental distinction in the kind of generalization of essence *(Wesensverall- gemeinerung)* as between "material *a priori*" and "formal *a priori*".

However, the distinction of the analytic *a priori* and the

synthetic *a priori* has not been drawn by Husserl in an entirely predicative context, as by Kant. Kant's distinction between analytic and synthetic statements refers primarily to judgments of the subject-predicate form, although it extends to the whole field of possible knowledge. Indeed Kant takes "analytic" in a narrower sense, as based merely on contradiction (or non-contradiction), whereas for Husserl the logic of truth, besides that of non-contradiction, is not to be excluded from the scope of formal logic. However, it should be noted that Husserl's distinction between the analytic and the synthetic in his critique of *a priori* knowledge appears ultimately to be motivated more by his radical transcendentalism than by purely *logical* considerations. (It is worth remembering in this connexion, that even Kant took the key in formulating his table of "categories" admittedly from the Aristotelian classification).

The Husserlian motive for "synthetic a priori" has to be sought for in the fundamental constructive task of his critique of logical principles – that of uncovering the presuppositions implicitly hidden in logical forms and rules. And that raises the problem of evidence and truth – one that is quite different from the problem of judgments as bare meanings. What Husserl calls "pure logical grammar" *(reinlogische Grammatik)* – introduced in his earlier work, "Logical Investigations" – is concerned with the doctrine of forms of meaning. And for a closer understanding of the essence of judgmental forms, a further distinction between "syntactical form" and "syntactical stuff" has been introduced. Syntax, which has its obvious relevance from the side of the grammarian, would signify in the "grammar of logic" a descriptive demonstration of the essence-structures of the sphere of judgment. (This is an evident departure from the logical empiricist programme of the "logical syntax of language".)

Thus we are led to the genuinely phenomenological problem of the genesis of meaning *(Sinnesgenesis)* in respect of judgments.[9] To consider the typical character of judgment from the phenomenological point of view, it is defined as a product of "constitution" or genesis. And owing to the peculiarity of the essence of such product, each meaning-form *(Sinnesgebilde)* comes into force

[10] Vide *Form. u. tr. Logik*, § 85.

according to the level of meaning essential to it. If mere syntactical implications are not adequate to provide clues towards the meanings which judgments represent, the origination of such meanings *qua* ideal essences has to be sought for in some deeper genesis. And what else could it be other than experience itself, from which the judgment springs?

Now, once it is admitted that the origination of the ideal essences of thought lies in experience, the path that seems to suggest itself to us is that of *psychological* analysis. Thus in the psychological orientation of logic in Hume's philosophy, logic is sought to be treated as a branch of the descriptive science of psychology. The place that is assigned to logic within psychology is defined by the faculty of "understanding" to which logic restricts itself. On closer consideration, one can point to two logics in Hume, as Passmore has shown, viz., the logic of Reason and the logic of Understanding.[11] Of these, the province of formal logic would lie with the so-called logic of Reason which deals with the theory of demonstration. And as Hume admits, formally valid reasoning from necessarily two premises would be possible in respect of mathematics alone.

So far as the other logic is concerned, viz., that of non-demonstrative reasoning, the method is causal inference, which is the essence of all empirical inference in general. Here, unlike in mathematical reasoning, there obtains no *formal* connexion between what is taken as *evidence* and what follows as conclusion. The question would naturally arise: if not a formal relation, what sort of relation, then, could be there as between evidence and conclusion? The Humean answer refers to a *psychological* rather than a *logical* necessity in the relation, i.e., in terms of a psychological description of the thinking process.

Now, in the light of the phenomenological meta-logic, the Humean critique of formal logic would suffer from a shortcoming deeper than the mere inner inconsistency – "an inner tension", to which Passmore refers – between the sceptical estimate of causal inference on the one hand and a belief in the "scientific" (in Hume's case, psychological) method on the other. It is the shortcoming of the fundamental *psychologistic* commitment that

[11] John Passmore, *Hume's Intentions*, ch. II.

Hume shares with other empiricists. The chief issue in the Husserlian polemic against psychologism – which latter Humeanism amply demonstrates – is that if the essential theoretic basis of logic lies in psychology; then logic would prove to be only a psychological discipline, so far as psychology should provide the theoretic basis for the construction of a logical theory.

The chief points on which Husserl meets psychologism are as follows.[12] (1) Psychology cannot yield more than *empirical* universals resulting from psychical phenomena, psychical dispositions and organic processes. That is why they cannot result in any apodictically evident, over-empirical *(über-empirisch)* and absolutely exact laws, which, after all, make out the very core of logic. (2) Laws of thought *(Denkgesetze)*, if defined as laws of nature, i.e., as causal laws, could only be formulated in terms of *probability;* and that would mean an extreme probabilism in all knowledge. To put it otherwise, psychologistic logic fails to recognize the fundamental distinction between *ideal* laws and *real* laws, between logical necessity and real (i.e. psychological) necessity. (3) If logical laws originated in psychological factualities, they would have psychological content – which would mean, they are laws of psychical phenomena and also include the psychically existent within their scope. But no logical laws as such imply matters of fact, nor the existence of actual psychical presentation. In other words, no logical law, strictly speaking, is to be treated as a law of the mental life. Further, on the contention of psychologistic logic (particularly, J. S. Mill) that judgmental forms are to be equated to the phenomena of inner experience, Husserl points out that in repeated *acts* of judging which are similar, the judgments formed and conclusions drawn are not merely similar but are numerically *identical*. (See Ch. II).

Against the psychologistic interpretation of logical forms – be it of the extreme Hume-Mill type, or be it of the continental positivists (Mach etc.), or even of Vaihinger (in his philosophy of "as if") – Husserl holds out his positive point, as supported by a phenomenological critique of knowledge. Thus Husserl points out that even when Hume seeks to interpret thought-forms through fictionalistic psychology and theory of knowledge, the

[12] Vide *Log. Unt.*, Vol. II.

nature of the said "fictions" themselves are not considered. Phenomenologically speaking, such fictions, considered as presentations to mind, must have their individual kinds of being *(Seinsart)* – their ways of being evident, their modes of givenness as unities in multiplicities. And Husserl emphatically asserts that the logical forms represent ideal objectivities as "transcendences"; and such ideality has to be understood in the light of "psychic irreality". As such, to psychologize the irreal meaning-forms *(irreale Bedeutungsgebilde)* would be obviously unwarranted.

VII

Towards a vindication of a "pure" logic as distinguished from psychology, the problem of "origination" has again to be considered. The point of departure for the Husserlian transcendental-logical problematic shows itself in this question of origin *(Ursprungsproblem)*.[13] The phenomenological explanation shows that the region of the logical, properly speaking, extends beyond that envisaged by traditional logic. For, such origin is traced to the grounds of essence which underly, as presuppositions, behind the meaning and value of the evidence with which logic is concerned. And as already evident, a phenomenological "genealogy of logic" has necessarily to depart from a genetic psychology of judgment.

From the point of view of *Sinnesgenesis*, or the origin of meaning – i.e., the latent "intentional implications" *(die verborgene intentionalen Implikationen)*, enclosed within the judgment itself as its form[14] – the transcendental critique of judgment proceeds in two major steps. (a) The unit of analysis is individual judgment, i.e., the narrow experiential judgment *(Erfahrungsurteil)*; thus the first theory of judgment is that of evident judgment which provides individual evidence of the narrowest form. (b) In a theory of evident judgment, again, the prior step is that of genetically tracing back the predicative evidence itself to the non-predicative evidence which is simply experience.[15] And this

---

[13] Cf. Husserl, *Erfahrung und Urteil*, Einleitung.
[14] *Form. u. tr. Log.*, § 85, p. 184.
[15] *Ibid.*, § 86.

turn-back to the evidence of the experiential judgments is not derived through any inductive experience *(Empirie)* of the psychological observer. Rather what is to be taken into consideration is the essence-status *(Wesensbestand)* of intentionality, constituting the nature of consciousness itself. Each kind of object for consciousness – whether idealities, universal truths or judgmental knowledge – has its way of givenness as "self-given evidence".

Formal logic has to do only with the forms of possible judgments and truths, but does not as such concern itself with the question of "evidence" in original experience. In its phase of subjective enquiry – as a critique of knowledge – into the radical method of intentional functionality, formal analytic has to take the categorial mediation of evidence into account. The origin of judgments in and through such functionality can thus be explained; for through the mediation of evidence alone can judgments be referred back to the original grounds of experience, in their modes of givenness. In its fundamental functionality experience presents modes of syntactical performance; only the latter are free from all the conceptual and grammatical formations which characterize the categorial purely in the context of predicative judgments.

So far as formal apophantic logic – and formal ontology too – are concerned, there remains a sort of phenomenological naivete regarding the real world as pregiven. Formal logic does not ask question about the distinctions in the way of pregivenness *(Vorgegebenheit)* of objects; it only asks about the conditions of evident judgments but not about the conditions of the evident *givenness* of the objects of judgment.[16] For Husserl, formal logic remains, after all, the logic meant for the real world thought as pregiven *(Logik für eine vorgegeben gedachte reale Welt)*. Unlike in formal logic, the phenomenological origin of judgment concerns the very evidence of the pregiven objects themselves, i.e., the conditions of the evident givenness of objects referred to in judgments.

So, to put the rationale of the so-called "transcendental logic" of Husserl, the logical forms are to be interpreted in the light of

---

[16] Cf. *Erfahrung und Urteil*, § 4.

the original functionality of consciousness in generating the ways of givenness of the forms concerned. This givenness – or rather, as Husserl would prefer to call it, "self-givenness" *(Selbstgebung)* – constitutes the evidence for the ideality of logical forms. Thus what Husserl calls the "original constitution" of the logical forms – that which constitutes the foundation of ideal objectivities, or foundation of meaning *(Sinnesfundament)*, of the logical kind – is to be sought for in the functionality and performing activity of consciousness. Nevertheless, such activity should not be taken as "creating" or "constructing" (in any idealistic sense) the ideal objects and imparting to them an ontological status as such. It only holds out the peculiar evidence, i.e., the intentional activity of self-giving *(die intentionale Leistung der Selbstgebung)*, as pertaining to the ideal objectivities of the logical kind.[17]

This search for direct evidence, in which the true meaning of logical principles *(der eigentliche und reine Sinn der logischen Prinzipien)* is grounded, calls for a deeper insight into the essence and structure of pre-predicative experience *(vorprädikative Erfahrung)*. Accordingly Husserl maintains that the demonstration of such pre-predicative evidence can primarily be found in the pre-scientific world of common experience – what is called *"Lebenswelt"* (q. v. Chs. VI & VIII). All predicative evidences are finally grounded on the evidence of experience. Thus in the world of lived experience alone do we encounter logical meanings – not, of course, as ready factors operating in judgments, but as original evidence constituting meaning. Consequently, the turn-back *(Rückgang)* to the world of experience in search of the ground of evidence for judgments would mean tracing back to the world of lived experience.[18]

Conclusion

To conclude, Husserl does not in any way mean to deny formal logic and its analytic region. What he denies is rather that the latter is self-explanatory, on ultimate analysis. Its final meaning,

---

[17] Categories of objectivity and categories of evidence are, according to Husserl, correlate; for each fundamental kind of objectivity belongs a fundamental kind of "experience" of evidence. ("Zu jeder Grundart von Gegenständlichkeiten ... gehört eine Grundart der 'Erfahrung', der Evidenz ..."). cf. *Form. u. tr. Log.*, p. 144.
[18] Vide *Erfahrung und Urteil*, § 7, 10.

on the contrary, has to be sought for in a new dimension, i.e., in the subjective direction of constitutive functionality out of consciousness (transcendental subjectivity). The transition from formal logic to transcendental logic marks the second- or higher-order problem in logic. Such a problem could be raised only when a deeper *theoretic* attitude prevails – one that demands clarification of the origin of judgments from the point of view of subjective (not psychological) grounds which are presupposed. So the relation between formal logic and transcendental logic is not to be understood as a disjunctive one – we cannot decide either for the one or for the other. One might, of course, stop with formal logic; but as Husserl remarks, transcendental logic is not to be looked upon as "a second logic", but is rather "the radical and concrete logic itself" – one that arises through the adoption of the phenomenological method.[19] In the latter case alone logic would be promoted from a mere apparatus of thought-functions to a full-fledged critique of experience.

---

[19] Cf. *Form. u. tr. Log.*, p. 256: ". . . die nicht eine zweite Logik, sondern nur die in phänomenologischer Methode erwachsende radikale und konkrete Logik selbst ist".

CHAPTER IV

SUBJECTIVISM IN PHENOMENOLOGY

"Subjectivism" or "subjective" is often used in philosophy in a more or less evaluative sense and rather disapprovingly. Thus, idealistic philosophy, for instance, in its primary phase has been charged by realists at large with subjectivism. The like charge of subjectivism is not unlikely to be brought against the new philosophical discipline of Phenomenology. And that may be partly because of its typical – and sometimes not unambiguous – outlook and method, and partly also because of misunderstanding with regard to its peculiarly non-committal standpoint. So it is worth examining the question whether and how far phenomenology can actually be called a *subjective* philosophy, i.e., a philosophy open to the charge of subjectivism – the latter being evidently taken in its narrow condemnatory sense. The later part of the Chapter (section 6 in particular) would further be concerned with the question in what sense does the principle of subjectivity play a central role in phenomenology.[1]

I

Subjectivism in philosophy roughly stands for a view which maintains that the truth of some class of statements depends on the mental states or reactions of the person making the statements. The question of subjectivism may be raised in respect of a philosophy principally on two aspects: method and resulting position. Thus a particular philosophy can be said to pursue a subjective method; and a philosophy can take a subjectivist

[1] The present Chapter is, however, more concerned with the first aspect of the question, viz., the polemical question posed here.

position as a result of its analysis and enquiry. The latter need not necessarily be dependent on the former, but the former may often lead to the latter position.

In Phenomenology, however, the method and point of view appears to be more important than the resulting thesis. And that is so chiefly because phenomenology, in its program, is not concerned with any metaphysical world-view as such, nor does it address itself to yielding a system of truths and principles regarding Being and its ontological character. It is a mode of analysis rather than a theory of reality. For, it attempts a new philosophical discipline which would, on the one hand, not admit of being reduced to any of the natural sciences, and would yet retain a non-metaphysical character in its freedom from pre-suppositions. In a sense, it should put up an *empirical* outlook which, however, need not remain *simply* empirical but rather adopts the method of reflection in its own rigorous field of enquiry. Our present enquiry, therefore, shall largely be directed towards a closer examination of the methodological subjectivism which, it is doubted, is involved in the very program of pheno-menological philosophy.

As regards the exact impact of subjectivism, several possible meanings can be formulated. The latter may pertain to the method as much as to the result – to any one of them, or to both, – because too rigid a distinction between these two aspects of philosophizing often appears to be an impossibility.

a) Subjectivism may simply mean *psychologism*. That is, to be subjective is to be psychologically determined. Whatever truth is asserted is so merely on the basis of psychological analysis and investigation of the mental states concerned. What actually happen in the mind are taken to be the standard in the light of which anything regarding the nature of reality can be stated. In the same measure, that which is not posited merely with reference to psychological foundation would be called "objective", i.e., non-psychological or non-mental.

b) Subjectivism, in the sense of individualism or relativism, holds truth to be merely *personal*, consequently varying from person to person and from case to case. This meaning, it is obvious, is closely analogous to the first one, and the two (a & b) may almost be regarded as emphasising respectively the two aspects of the same truth – what is personal is empirically a psychological entity and what is psychological is at the same time personal. Thus, we usually go to reject the claim to truth of anything that is put forward on "merely personal reasons".

c) Coming to the more philosophical orientation of subjectivism, particularly in the epistemological context, we may point to what in general is regarded as the subjective standpoint, which is often characterized as "ego-centric". This ego-centricity implies the necessary dependence of the epistemic object upon the cognizing subject, not taking the *personal* constitution of the latter into consideration. In this sense, to be subjective would mean dependence upon the subject principle, due concession being given to the possible variability of both the factors (viz., object and subject) – only the former, i.e., the object, would be dependent upon the latter. Thus, for instance, dream objects are taken to be subjective so far as they are essentially dependent upon the dreaming consciousness and as such described to be "private". Corresponding to this notion of subjectivity, the *objective* would be that which is not determined by any possible connection with a subject, and as such can be regarded as independent and "public". The "public" facts accordingly lay claim to validity over "private" facts, the latter broadly covering all the three senses of subjectivity recorded here.

d) Further, there may be a slightly wider meaning of subjectivity in the sense of relatedness or reference to the subject-principle – a sense under which the element of subject-dependence may be considered. To be essentially related to the subject or to bear reference to it need not mean to be necessarily dependent on the subject. But to be dependent – whether completely or partially – upon a subject would necessarily mean to be related to, or to have essential reference to, the subject. To have a particular "perspective" (visual) of a thing or a landscape would be *subjective*, not in the sense of being dependent upon the observer but (in the sense) that it can occur only in the context of the perceiver, i.e., in relation to the perceiving mind. A realist, like B. Russell, however, extends this notion of "perspective" further towards an objectivistic orientation so as to define the physical object in terms of a "system of perspectives". Dream-objects, which would generally be admitted as phenomena entirely dependent on the perceiving (i.e. dreaming) mind, seem in this sence to be only a special case of subject-relatedness; but unlike the visual perspective, a dream object cannot be described as merely related to the subject, being *totally* – not partially – dependent on the latter.

II

Turning now to Husserl's Phenomenology, we come across a methodological approach which is admittedly subjective; and phenomenology, offering a new rigorous discipline, would be nothing if its methodology for philosophic reflection is left apart. But it is to be examined how far, and in which of the senses enumerated above, can phenomenological method be treated as *subjective*. In the preface to his "Ideas" (trans. B. Gibson), Husserl writes: "Turning inwards in pure reflexion, following exclusively 'inner experience' and setting aside all the psycho-physical questions which relate to man as a corporeal being, I obtain an original and pure descriptive knowledge of the psychical life as it is in itself, the most original being obtained from myself, because here alone is perception the medium".[2] Starting with this statement but before proceeding further, it may be advisable at this stage to draw a clear distinction between two different kinds of phenomenology, which mark respectively the earlier and the later phases of its development.

The central, and also the later phase, of phenomenology can generally be labelled as *transcendental* phenomenology, which further goes to make for what Husserl calls *transcendental idealism*. Here the expression "transcendental" means to characterize the presuppositional status of consciousness in which the phenomena, which present themselves as beyond the region of consciousness, are *intended* or meant by the consciousness, whose essential character lies in referentiality. As distinguished from this trancendental form of phenomenology, the earlier phase is non-transcendental and takes the shape of a purely *descriptive phenomenology*, which does not necessarily tend to any pronounced idealism. On the contrary, such phenomenology was aimed at

---

[2] *Ideas*. Vol. I. Preface (tr. B. Gibson).

providing a basis for empirical psychology and the sources out
of which the fundamental concepts and the ideal laws of pure
logic arise. In his "Logical Investigations", Husserl developed a
descriptive phenomenology of intentional consciousness in which
the bi-polar structure of intentionality – in terms of the *intending*
acts and of the *intended* objects – were studied, without committing
himself to any particular pole as such.

III

Now, as against the first two senses of subjectivism enumerated
above, viz., psychologism and individual relativism, phenomenology seems to present a markedly anti-psychologistic viewpoint. In his "Logical Investigations" Husserl presents his critique
of psychologism. The motive behind this critique was to indicate
a new logic, claiming to be pure and free from the approach of
empirical psychology. The inadequacy of a purely psychological
basis for *ideal* laws, as distinguished from *real* laws, was shown.
Husserl argued that psychology cannot give more than empirical
universals, drawn from psychical phenomena, psychical exposi-
tions and organic processes. That is why psychologists cannot give
any apodictically evident non-empirical, exact laws which should
constitute the core of pure logic.

Further, the phenomenological standpoint marks a sharp point
of departure from that of empirical psychology. The difference
between the psychological and the phenomenological descriptions of inner experience has been repeatedly stressed by Husserl
– both the disciplines being concerned with what superficially
appears to be the same subject-matter. While psychology is a
science of *facts*, of natural events (even though mental), presented
to the observer, phenomenology proposes to be a science not of
facts but of "essential being" or "essences". To stress the point of
distinction further, psychology is concerned with *real* events
phenomena that are, after all, empirical and world-involved,
having spatio-temporal location. The contents of phenomenological investigation, on the other hand, are to be characterized
not as *real* but rather as non-real or "irreal", as Husserl expresses
it. In psychology mind is directed upon experience under the

dictates of the "natural attitude" – dealing with some inner state of mind as a *natural* event having some physico-physiological correlate. The phenomenological point of view, on the contrary, concerns itself with the autonomous region of pure consciousness as disconnected from the natural order.

Thus it may at least here be contended that phenomenology is not essentially concerned with the phenomenon of subjectivity as factually belonging to a human person. This is, moreover, the point which drives Husserl to oppose the Heideggerian orientation of subjectivity in the light of his (Heidegger's) analysis of human existence *(Daseinsanalytik)* as involving "anthropologism". What Husserl strictly means by "transcendental subjectivity", non-anthropological and non-psychological as it is, may be discussed on some other occasion.

A similar predicament of psychologistic explanation may arise also when we come to consider more closely the exact status of "phenomena". In the phenomenological approach what stand as *facts* in the "natural attitude" are to be interpreted in terms of "phenomena", i.e., the meanings of objects *qua* meant by the subject. (No negative metaphysic of phenomena, distinguished from the real or "thing-in-itself", as in Kant, is implied). But are such "phenomena" to be understood as psychical, necessarily amenable to introspection? That the said "phenomena" are not to be understood in psychological terms would be evident from the very nature of the phenomenological analysis itself. For the latter proceeds with reference to intentional consciousness. And intentionality means the objectivating function of consciousness, and as such, intentional analysis should offer an interpretation of *objectivity*. The said function, again, in its elementary form, indicates that the subject (of consciousness) is confronted with *ideal* unities (or meaning), which in their turn stand as indentifiable.[3] In so analyzing objectivity in terms of the structure of intentionality, Husserl attempts to fight psychologism.

The point raised here is, of course, inevitably linked up with

---

[3] Cf. Remarks of Aron Gurwitsch, a critical exponent of phenomenology: "Objectivity is identifiableness, i.e., the possibility of reverting again and again to what, through the present experienced act, is offered to consciousness, and the possibility of so doing whether in the sense or in any other mode of awareness". A. Gurwitsch, "On the Intentionality of Consciousness" in *Philosophical Essays in memory of Edmund Husserl*, ed. M. Farber.

the question of the mode of apprehension of the said phenomena. The possibility of simple introspection in respect of them has been shelved (as mentioned already), and in its place the so-called "eidetic intuition" or "essence-intuition" is put forward as the positive method of phenomenological investigation. Through "essence-intuition" *(Wesensanschauung)* the "essence" – obviously distinguished from the actual *existence* of object, real or ideal, whose essence is sought to be intuited – is to be grasped in its pure being. That is how the individual appearances in which the essence represents itself can be held before consciousness – "before our eyes", as they would say. In so explaining the phenomena and the mode of their apprehension, phenomenology necessarily takes its point of departure from psychology. However, this problem brings us at once to one of the central issues in phenomenology, viz., the status of the intuited essence *vis-a-vis* intuition itself – an issue which has a close bearing on the last two aspects of subjectivism mentioned above.

IV

To turn now to the more philosophical – or rather, epistemological – orientation of subjectivism, it concerns the form of egocentricity. This, of course, relates to the issue of subject-dependence so far as the essences of phenomenological intuition are concerned. In this connexion the peculiar status of the essences (or what are sometimes called "phenomena") as *given* in phenomenological intuition or reflexion is to be considered. Thus, on the one hand, essences are acknowledged to be *given* to the reflecting consciousness *qua* universal object-meanings, the logical-objective status of which has been sought to be demonstrated in Husserl's earlier work, "Logical Investigations". The descriptive analysis, carried on in the said work of Husserl, proceeded in a rather neutral attitude, i.e., without any pronounced preference for either the subjective or the objective side. This phase of phenomenology – generally known as "descriptive phenomenology" (or sometimes as "non-transcendental" one) – is concerned with the descriptive study of the phenomena in their essential structures and has been widely interpreted as a "movement towards objectivity"

(Passmore) or as "a turn to the object".[4]

Now, so far as the question of the dependence of phenomena on the (empirical) subject is concerned, phenomenology would indeed answer in the negative. Firstly, there cannot be factual dependence on the part of the essences, for the latter are not facts but non-facts. Nor could there be epistemic dependence, for essences are not constructed but admittedly presented to the reflecting consciousness.

But here, again, comes into view the more important aspect of phenomenology as *transcendental*. It should be noted that essences or phenomena appear to have validity not in the absolutely *objective* context but essentially with reference to the reflecting consciousness itself. For, what would be the status of intuited essences apart from intuition itself? Now Husserl's position on the point has been set forth rather unambiguously: intentionality is not created through reflection. Intentionality, on the contrary, should *precede* its recognition through reflexion. As typically stated by Husserl: Reflexion enables intentionality to become clear to itself *(sich selbst klar werden)*. Thus consciousness, through the act of reflexion, does not *create* objects: rather consciousness, so to say, *becomes* objects – and so, not as things of the natural attitude but as appearances in meaning consciousness in which object-meanings are constituted.

So Husserl's phenomenology does not seem to involve subjectivism in the sense of dependence on empirical subject. But this does not preclude the possibility of phenomena being subject-dependent on a different level. For phenomenology, all phenomena are taken to be dependent on the *transcendental* subject as sharply distinguished from the empirical. This evidently brings us to the last, and wider, meaning of subjectivism as relatedness or reference to the subject principle. That phenomenology in its descriptive phase, as already noted, reveals no evidence for the necessary dependence of phenomena upon the empirical subject has to be taken into consideration in this context.

However, the dismissal of such subject-dependence of phenomena in the sense mentioned need not rule out the possibility that they are essentially subject-related. Phenomenology, as

---

[4] Cf. John Passmore in *A Hundred Years of Philosophy*. Ch. VIII.

basically the study of phenomena, cannot deny the truism that a phenomenon is essentially what appears to some one. And as Husserl defines it, what is, i.e., what we call existent, comes forth into appearance in the *phenomenon*. So a phenomenon has to be understood necessarily in the context of the reflexion of consciousness which *means* the object. The object for the phenomenologist is indeed not the naïve or natural object but always the object *as meant*, i.e., object-as-to-the-meaning-consciousness. In this sense, an underlying subjective element can hardly be denied in phenomenology – an element which comes to stay in transcendental phenomenology in spite of the apparently contrary trend in the earlier phase.

This deeper element of subjectivity may be explicitly understood with reference to the typical notion of "constitution" – a key concept in transcendental phenomenology. Following upon the descriptive analysis in terms of intentional consciousness and in search of a radical foundation and precondition of all knowledge-of-object, Husserl comes upon the method of "phenomenological reduction". It means tracing all phenomena back to subjectivity, or rather transcendental subjectivity, which provides the irreducible centre of reference for all objectivity. In the transcendental subject Husserl believes to have explored the foundational principle in which all intentional acts rest, on ultimate analysis. And the latter again, *constitute* the world of objectivity through their essential constitutive function. Consequently, the sense in which subjectivity can be said to constitute the object of knowledge is not that of bestowing the stuff of such object but rather as investing sense or meaning to the phenomena as the Husserlian expression *"sinngebende"* puts it. And what else would be the essence of phenomena apart from this element of sense or meaning?[5]

To assess in brief the role of phenomenological reduction one may point to, after Thévenaz,[6] a keen student of phenomenology, a twofold purpose that such reduction can serve. On the one hand, it should prevent a naive-realistic or naturalistic commit-

---

[5] Merleau-Ponty lays emphasis on the point, in a slightly different form: "The phenomenological world is not the bringing to explicit expression of a pre-existing being, but the laying down of being". Preface, *Phenomenology of Perception*.

[6] Cf. Pierre Thévenaz, *What is Phenomenology?*, ed. & trans. James Edie.

ment – the natural attitude being its very point of departure. On the other hand, reduction can fight all movement towards relativism chiefly rooted in the psychologistic predisposition, and thus make way for the apodictic evidence for the radical foundation of meaning. However, more positively considered, phenomenological reduction is aimed at the principle of transcendental subjectivity itself, the seat of all "world-constitution", on the last analysis.

Ambitious as the latter trend appears to be, it may further provoke the question as to how far constitutive phenomenology (sometimes even referred to as "absolute phenomenology") could be regarded as free from relativism and subjectivism. Now, is this said subjectivity, alleged to be the foundation of all objectivity, nay, of the intersubjective world of experience and science, to be understood with reference to a particular subject (as the case may be)? A definition of subjectivity in terms of individual subject would no doubt impart a relativistic basis to the said world-constitution. But such misunderstanding is not likely to gain ground if we take into account the fundamentally aprioristic attitude of phenomenology. The latter never offers to be an empirical study of consciousness in its empirical associations. Rather its aim is to study the *ideal* structure of consciousness in terms of *a priori* essences or idealities grounded therein. Husserl's interest lies primarily in the possible system of essences in terms of which the nature and structure of objectivity is to be interpreted. Consciousness as the ground of such object-constituting essences has necessarily been conceived as identical, no question of personal variation coming into forefront.

Even if there be a multiplicity of transcendental subjects – and there need not be any reason why it should not be so, – the underlying identity of the presuppositional principle of consciousness or subjectivity would still be there. The uniform constitution of human reason in its *a priori* essence serves no doubt as the unfailing working presupposition. Here a close resemblance to Kant, with his "transcendental *a priori*" of human reason (and its essential functional forms), may be observed.[7]

[7] Cf. Herbert Spiegelberg. "How subjective is Phenomenology?" *Proceedings of the American Catholic Philosophical Association*, 1959. (Our present theme has more particularly been suggested by this article under reference and the author owes to it certain points raised here.)

V

So far one point seems to be clear: phenomenology, though free from subjectivism in the sense of subject-dependence, does not dispense with the element of subject-relatedness (keeping "transcendental subjectivity" in view). The question may still legitimately be raised as to how far transcendental subjectivity can yield a strictly identical system, a systematic science of consciousness, not vitiated by the variability of individual consciousness. But to this we have already noted that Husserl drives at a truly universal subjective *a priori*.

This factor of subject-relatedness has again to be considered in the context of the phenomenological procedure itself. Thus the question: can the subjective association be altogether eliminated in the approach of the phenomenologist in terms of "evidence"? Whether in phenomenological description or induction, the self-evident intuition of the phenomena is claimed to provide the basis of judgment. For phenomenology, every type of first-hand intuition as the mode of the originally given consciousness provides the essential "source of authority" *(Rechtsquelle)*. But does the phenomenologist's appeal to *evidence* sufficiently protect itself against the verdict of individual consciousness? The alleged self-evidence of phenomena seems to contain, at least *prima facie*, a factor of contingency and arbitrariness. As Spiegelberg aptly remarks: "There is no bureau that grants phenomenological licenses, not even to self-declared phenomenologists".[8] Moreover, there might also be the possibility of spurious self-evidence or pseudo-evidence.

Now an answer to such a charge against the approach through evidence may provisionally be gained in a more cautious and self-critical application of the method of evidence. More and more approximation to the standard of objectivity (in the common "public" sense) in respect of the evidence of phenomena may possibly be gained in twofold directions. Firstly, the reflecting (that is, reduction-performing) mind has to be sharply dissociated from its psychological as well as intellectual conditions – a procedure which should, nevertheless, prove to be no

[8] *ibid.*

easier than the allied attitude of "bracketing" of natural belief in the world (i.e., phenomenological "Epoché"). Secondly, a larger degree of intersubjectivity and freedom from personal variability could also be obtained – more as a supplementary process – by recourse to a method commonly adopted in respect of the data of natural science. What I mean here is the process of subjecting the given of intuitive evidence to some sort of test through comparison of different evidences. Thereby we seek to grasp what is essential in the self-given phenomenon and eliminate what is non-essential and non-universal about it.

When empiricists – more particularly, logical empiricists – criticize the phenomenological method of evidence, they are apt to overlook "the fact that the intersubjective harmony implicit in the concept of *objectivity* has a highly complex structure", as Kaufmann, a critical exponent of Phenomenology, points out.[9] Logical empiricists and positivists, with their attention fixed on the idea of objectively given sense-data, in themselves irreducible and ultimate, would miss the question: What pressuppositions are implicit in the idea of an objective world of experience, and how are these presuppositions involved in the individual's experience of the world? The phenomenological method of evidence, on the other hand, aims at making explicit certain classes of presuppositions which were implicit in our common ideas about the objective world. And phenomenological evidence is *objective* in the senses that it forms the condition of the evident givenness (or rather, self-givenness) of the objects of judgment – the way in which an object can be marked in consciousness in its original givenness as "itself there".

Here it may be pointed out that the empirical and linguistic philosophers in their turn also refer to some sort of evidence, viz., *empirical evidence*. They would, in broad, agree that the constitution of the physical world has ultimately to be put in terms of sense-data even if indirectly. The world of material things, if not directly analysable into sense-data, is at least to be understood as a "construction" out of "our resources of sense-data". In other words, sense-data provide the kind of evidence by which the "physical object" statements are sought to be verified.

[9] F. Kaufmann. "Phenomenology and Logical Empiricism", *Philosophical Essays in memory of Edmund Husserl* (ed. M. Farber).

The question may still be raised: the objective data of sense-experience to which empiricists appeal are, as they claim, "public facts" – in contradistinction from which the evidence of eidetic intuition would appear to be "private". But the counter-question may as well be put: how far has the exact status of sense-data, in relation to physical objects, been unambiguously decided even in empirical philosophy itself? How to define this status of sense-data, taking the observing sensory agent into consideration? Sense-data are no doubt regarded as extra-mental, but yet recognised to be in some way relative to the observer. In fact, the perplexity which G. E. Moore pointed out in connexion with the status of sense-data, viz., the confusion between "the existence of the sensible which we experience and the fact that experience them", seems hardly to be overcome. However, the realistic instinct in Moore – and any hard empiricist – persuades him to believe that "the fact that our experience of a given sensible depends upon the condition of our nervous system does not strictly show that the existence of the sensible experienced always so depends".

On the other hand, we find Bertrand Russell, with all his realistic zeal, admit that although sense-data do not depend for their existence on something mental, they are yet "subjective" in a wider sense, insofar as they exist only in relation to a human nervous system. And to counter this vestige of subjectivism, Russell had to assert that physical objects are not, after all, sets of sense-data and as such should not be regarded as dependent on our nervous sytem. His introduction of "sensibilia" over and above sense-data points to the same direction of fighting the inner ambiguity involved in the idea of sense-data.

All these attempts at defining the rather perplexing status of sense-data only go to point out the truism that even an empirical-realistic explanation of the world in terms of empirical evidence cannot be so free from the subjective element as it claims to be. So, why should phenomenology be at fault – at least on this ground? It offers, on the contrary, to be more consistently true to evidence, so far as it shelves the element of existentiality. Its analysis, after all, proceeds not in terms of facts but of non-factual essences. Phenomena or essences are no doubt *meant* – and to that extent, bear relation to the meaning subject. But to call them "meant" does not imply their being *subjective*. They should rather be called *objective*, so far as they are based on the laws of meaning. And such meaning is quite different from what is arbitrary or what one simply wants the object to be. For the former bears essential reference to the universal precondition of objectivity.

VI

The polemical questions concerning subjectivism in phenomenology being so far treated, we may now further raise the positive question as to how subjectivity is to be understood in the phenomenological philosophy – the role of that principle in the latter. In the foregoing sections we have discussed how the phenomenological explanation of knowledge and objects does not entail subjectivism in the empirical-psychological sense. That much of subject-relatedness which it implies need not as such make it particularly vulnerable to the charge of subjectivism. Nor, on the other hand, should subjectivity be treated as reducible in terms of linguistic analysis and usage. For that would go against the very nature of the phenomenological method and outlook. (See Ch. II).

Hence the point of departure in search of the phenomenological principle of subjectivity can well be provided by the so-called distinction between empirical and transcendental subjectivity. The concept of the latter is admittedly adopted by Husserl directly from the Kantian conception of the same. However positively it may otherwise be characterized, the definite point about it is that it is non-empirical (or rather, over-empirical). For whatever is empirical, i.e., a fact of experience, must be amenable to the process of phenomenological reduction or disconnection. But the so-called "transcendental subjectivity" is the one principle which appears to stand all phenomenological disconnections; it proves to be that on which, as Husserl contends, reduction can have no grip.

That could be so only because subjectivity (if we may so term it in want of any other nominal expression) is presupposed, and as such inescapable, in every act of knowing. It is not given as such in the conscious act itself; nevertheless it is the precondition for the possibility of such acts or situations. Therefore the best way to characterize it would rather be to call it "transcendental" (after Kant); for therebe alone its presuppositional and functional status in relation to knowledge and experience could be indicated.

One possibility here, however, might perhaps be to treat such alledge non-empirical subjectivity as nothing more than a *nominal* construction, having no content for itself. Be it in Humean associationism, be it in Ryle's analytical neo-behaviorism, empiricists would prefer to treat subjectivity practically as an "index term" – as a pseudo-concept which may hide within itself the "systematic elusiveness" (Ryle in *the Concept of Mind*) about the so-called I-object. For the phenomenologist, however, the approach to the question would be completely different. For him the contents of phenomenological analysis have their being (essence-wise, as it is) only as referred to the "subjective life of consciousness itself".

This "subjective life of consciousness" stands for the region of *purified* experience – purified so far as it is "disconnected" from the actual world of facts. As such, the said region – non-factual, *ideal* as it is – is not be equated with the psychological region or the complex of mental states. Indeed Husserl has definitely decided for the term "consciousness" to mean subjectivity – and would even use the expression "pure consciousness" to be more clear about the import of phenomenological subjectivity. Accordingly "transcendental" also has been defined as "the quality of that which is consciousness".[10]

However, it can hardly be denied that the term "consciousness" so used seems inevitably to carry with it a suggestion of an entitative principle. Would it mean going back upon the "Cartesian myth" concerning spiritual substance? Whether posited as substantive or not, Husserl's contention regarding to presuppositional status of consciousness seems to be quite unambiguous. "Pure consciousness", he states, "has the absolute priority in relation to which all being is *aposteriori*".[11] Indeed to define further this "absolute priority" itself would be an embarassing task for a strict phenomenologist. Either one has actually to

---

[10] Husserl's Article on "Phenomenology" in *Encyclopaedia Britannica* (14th Ed.).
[11] *Ideen;* Vol. III, Sec. 12.

define it in absolute terms, i.e., existentially posit as absolute; but that would obviously be a non-phenomenological approach. Or, on the other hand, keeping to the limits of phenomenological reflection, one may adopt the strictly "functional" point of view, which Husserl himself recommends.[12] In accordance with the latter alternative, which is admittedly phenomenological, the preference would rather go in favour of the typically non-committal definition of consciousness as the "phenomenological residuum". For, after all, the "functional problem" is concerned with, according to Husserl, how "all fundamental types of consciousness and the modification, fusion, syntheses which essentially belong to them" may be systematically studied "in their eidetic generality and phenomenological purity".[13]

At this stage, however, the question of the ontological status of the alleged "transcendental subjectivity" or consciousness (the latter concept being apparently more suggestive of an ontological status) would naturally arise. Leaving the question to be decided in the context of the general question regarding ontological commitment in phenomenology (see chapter VI), certain observations may be offered here.

1) In the phenomenological analysis, the object is not the bare existent, but that which is *meant* by the subject. In other words, the being of an object *(Gegenstandsein)* is the "intentional correlate".

2) But to be an "intentional correlate" would necessitate a system within which it holds good; and such a system is "accomplished" (i.e., constituted) by subjectivity. For intentionality is functionality – "accomplishing functionality" *(Leistung)* – which signifies the dynamic transition from "empty" consciousness to "filled" consciousness.

3) Consequently, in the light of phenomenological reduction to transcendental consciousness, the scope of objectivity is to be viewed as the accomplishing functionality of transcendental consciousness. And that would point to the need for admitting the so-called "accomplishing subjectivity" *(leistende Subjek-*

---

[12] Cf. "The viewpoint of Function is the Central viewpoint of Phenomenology", *Ideas*, Vol. I, p. 252 (trans. B. Gibson).
[13] Vide *ibid.*, p. 253.

tivität) – one that is ultimately to be recognized, following the trend of phenomenological interpretation, as "world-constituting" *(weltkonstituierend)*.

From the last point in particular it would further follow that if the principle of subjectivity is to be taken as the seat of all world-meanings, and as such the ultimate precondition of all meaning of being *(Seinssinn)*, then such a principle seems naturally to demand to be posited in unconditionally *existential* terms. Indeed Husserl tends towards an existential assertion of the foundational principle of consciousness – particularly in the form of "pure Ego". As to the latter concept, however, its exact nature and status in relation to consciousness seem to require particular examination. (See Ch. V). For the question may well be raised whether the phenomenological account of consciousness, strictly speaking, could at all leave any room for an egological conception, i.e., a view of consciousness necessarily entailing the pure ego or "I".

Leaving to the next chapter the problem of connecting consciousness to ego, we may as well sum up the phenomenological position concerning subjectivity by referring to Husserl's recurrent note of recognizing the foundational principle of subjectivity. Whether a metaphysical reality or not, the *autonomous* status of consciousness would follow from its presuppositional character itself. To be "transcendental" would imply at least a possible autonomy for subjectivity or consciousness in relation to all empirical complex to which it can refer without itself being empirical. Husserl admits that there is, on final analysis, something about consciousness which cannot be intellectually manipulated. And he confessedly declares: "Pure I and pure consciousness is the wonder of all wonders".[14]

Yet such an admission of mystery about consciousness need not be taken to demonstrate an attitude of agnostic negativism in phenomenology. On the contrary Husserl is not even ready to admit that consciousness can be treated as a mere title name for psychical complexes. Negatively considered, consciousness is not be taken as a nominal or conceptual construction or a deri-

---

[14] "Das Wunder aller Wunder ist reines Ich und reines Bewusstsein", *Ideen* III, Sec. 12; also see Ch. VIII, 3. 4.

vative concept; for transcendental subjectivity does not signify a product of speculative constructions. But Husserl takes up an unmistakably positive attitude in asserting that "it is consciousness through and through, the source of all reason and unreason, all right and wrong, all reality and illusion, all value and disvalue, all deed and misdeed".[15] Taking into view its fundamentally presuppositional character and at the same time keeping to the typical non-committal attitude of phenomenology, transcendental subjectivity can, after all, be described as "an absolutely self-subsistent autonomous region of direct experience".[16]

[15] *Ideas*, Vol. I, p. 251 (English trans.).
[16] *Ideen* III, Nachwort, p. 141.

CHAPTER V

CONCEPT OF PERSON AND SUBJECTIVITY [1]

Reviewing the phenomenological position in respect of subjectivity – as in the preceding chapter – two questions seem to emerge with particular acuteness, and need clarification. One is with regard to the possibility of final characterization of the ontological status of consciousness – a question we prefer to keep in abeyance till the more general one regarding ontological commitment in Phenomenology is dealt with (see Chapter VII). The other question concerns, as already noted in the last chapter, the problem of identifying – or rather, relating – the principle of transcendental subjectivity with the actual human subject that is a person. In the latter case it has moreover to be decided whether the phenomenological view of pure consciousness would necessarily assume an "egological" character or should remain in the long run *non-egological*. Whatever alternative may be found finally acceptable, the relation between the so-called "transcendental ego" and the factual I or ego as ordinarily understood, has in any case to be shown. But that would entail a phenomenological analysis and description of the ego taken as a fact. So we come upon an investigation, on phenomenological lines, into the nature of *person* – the concept representing the facthood of human *I*, the rational self-conscious individual, who at the same time acts purposively.

I. *Possibility of a phenomenology of person*

The notion of person occupies a curious position in the discourse of Husserl's phenomenology. As with all facts and objects,

[1] Adapted from the author's article: "Der Begriff der Person in der Phänomenologie Husserls", pub. in *Zeitschrift für philosophische Forschung*, October 1964.

the facthood of person also is treated in the phenomenological attitude as a "phenomenon", (i.e., the essential meaning of an object for consciousness, obtained by systematically "neutralizing" the factual character of existent objects). But unlike other objects and facts, personality bears a unique inseparable relation to the subject principle – as may be evident on primary reflection, whatever be the exact nature of the relation concerned. Subjectivity, again, has pivotal significance in the phenomenological analysis. Consequently, a paradox seems to arise which may briefly be put thus: person is an object for phenomenological investigation, and is at the same time a presupposition of the latter.

At the outset, however, a question may be put: can there be at all a phenomenology of personality? Phenomenologically viewed, all that is "transcendent", i.e., all that falls beyond the range of the immanently evident in consciousness, is to be bracketed out. In that case, "bracketing" should also hold good of the fact that is person (and personal life). Psychology, as the science of the mental *(Wissenschaft des Seelischen)*, has been excluded from the scope of phenomenology on the same ground. Yet Husserl maintains that the fact of personality and mentality does in a sense come within the sphere of immanent givenness too. Thus, on his own admission, ". . . there is a phenomenology of man, of his personality, of his personal characteristics and his (human) stream of consciousness".[2]

The phenomenological interpretation of personality should not in any case pertain to the dimension of existential being – or as Heidegger would put it, "the dimension of the question as to the being of existence" *(Sein des Daseins)*.[3] Husserl would agree with Max Scheler in *not* posing the question with regard to the "being of person" *(Person-Sein)*. According to Scheler, person cannot be viewed either as a thing or as a substance; it is rather "the immediately and innerly felt *unity* of experiencing" *(die unmittelbar miterlebte Einheit des Erlebens)*. Person is thus not to be posited as a thing which is thought to be behind and besides the immediately experienced.[4]

Thus the existential aspect of personhood does not exactly

---

[2] *Ideen* I, p. 142.
[3] M. Heidegger, *Sein und Zeit*, p. 47.
[4] Scheler, *Der Formalismus in der Ethik und die materiale Wertethik*, p. 382.

come within the purview of a phenomenological enquiry. Even substantiality, as spoken of as a general category with reference to things and objects, would be denied of person in the context of phenomenological explanation. All that can be admitted in the explanation of personhood is the principle of *unity* – one that may serve as the substrate for the different psychological properties in the similar way as a substance is the substrate of qualities. But this unity evidently differs from that of the things of nature – it is "constituted" essentially in a different way (to put it from the point of view of "regional constitution", q.v. below). For the said unity is to be understood essentially in the context of "stream of experience" *(Strom des Erlebnisses)*. As Husserl remarks, person is "the unified pole of identity, the substrate of character and such like"; but all that refers back to the stream of experience.[5]

Again the very fact that the person evolves, distinguishes him from physical things. The way in which *I* can be comprehended as the substrate of properties, which are supposed to belong to *I*, is quite different from that in which thing is experienced as the substrate of its states and properties. For the thing has to be viewed as the substrate of properties which abide in their natural causal relation. The unity of the person, on the other hand, is to be understood with reference to its own "temporal life" *(zeitliches Leben)*.

In further exposition of this unity Husserl refers to a twofold polarity – I-pole on the one side and the object as the counterpole *(Gegenpol)* on the other. Each of the poles has its own type of identity. Thus the I is the identical subject of functions in all acts of the same "stream of consciousness"; it is the "centre of emanations" *(Ausstrahlungszentrum)*, so to say. The unity of the object also is in a sense to be understood in the context of reference-acts. While all acts of reference unite in the unifying subject, they are not so in the object of reference, or the object referred to; in the latter only such acts are united which can be viewed as "consciousness of" the self-same object.[6]

---

[5] Cf. "Person ist zwar einheitlicher Identitätspol, Substrat für Charakter und dergleichen, aber das alles weist zurück auf den Strom des Erlebnisses". – Husserl, *Manuskript* A VI 15.
[6] Cf. *Ideen* II, § 25.

II. *The natural and the personal*

The constitution of the mental personal world is generally distinguished by Husserl from the constitution of the physical world.[7] Thus nature is defined by Husserl as "a sphere of bare things" *(eine Sphäre blosser Sachen)*, a sphere of objectivities.[8] Separated from all value predicates and practical predicates, nature presents as such a sphere of "theoretical interest". And this attitude of viewing things signifies an abstraction from all references to human values and usefulness, and approves the observation of things only in their spatio-temporal material character.

So a twofold distinction of attitudes in the interpretation of facts and experience – namely, the naturalistic and the personalistic – comes into view, corresponding to the two worlds of nature and of spirit (in the broadly accepted sense) respectively. The former relates to the ego that is a person (i.e., personal I) and his *personal* world, yielding a theory of personality or egology as well as a social theory. And the latter concerns the natural-scientific theory of mind *(Seelenlehre)*. Accordingly Husserl speaks of moral or mental science as the "personal science" *(personale Wissenschaft)*, which grows along with the growth of theoretic interest in the person as such, i.e., in the personal life as personal.[9] That attitude is called by Husserl "personalistic" or pertaining to "mental science" *(Geisteswissenschaft* – Husserl adopts the concept, in distinction from "natural science", as introduced by Wilhelm Dilthey) which is directed to the human ego (i.e., I), to persons and the world effected by persons (the mental world, in other words).[10]

While natural science explains in terms of external causality, mental or moral science *(Geisteswissenschaft)* appeals to a unique type of causality, viz., the "intentional". In the latter context, the fundamental structure of consciousness which lies in the

---

[7] The reference here is to the typical problem of "regional constitution" in transcendental phenomenology – i.e., the original formation of meaning *(ursprüngliche Sinnbildung)* in respect of a "region" or group of objects of systematic experience, meant in their unity. See below, Ch. VI, 3; also below, sec. 4.

[8] *Ibid.*, § 11.

[9] Cf. Beilage XIII, *Phänomenologische Psychologie*, Husserliana IX.

[10] Cf. Husserl, MS. A V 7.

subjective act of reference is taken into consideration. In the light of this referentiality alone does phenomenology seek to interpret the immanent objectivity of the given in consciousness. Thus instead of the natural-mechanical interpretation of physical events, the phenomena that come within the scope of personalistic study are to be considered *qua* immanent objectivity, with necessary reference to subjectivity that acts. So viewed, the mind works upon the surrounding world by way of intentionality through the medium of the body and is also affected by the world to that extent; it deals with things *subjectively* through bodily operations. In this case mind is looked upon as the principle underlying all so-called *personal* phenomena – the abiding substrate of the properties of character, personal habits etc. As such it is to be sharply differentiated from the mental ego, which is a part of nature and to that extent constitutes the theme of the natural science of psychology. Consequently, the two aspects of I are to be clearly distinguished – the mental I, which is a part of nature, and the I as *person*, a member of the social-spiritual world to which he belongs.

In pursuance of this distinction between the natural I and the personal I, Husserl further brings out the different possible steps in the phenomenological investigation into the constitution of ego in its dual phases as natural and as personal.[11]

a) Mind is a presupposition even for the purely naturalistic attitude. From the point of view of natural sciences mind is "nothing for itself"; it rather indicates a bare level of real events in the body. To put it plainly, mind ensouls the body; and the ensouled body is a natural object within the spatio-temporal world.

b) Localisation of the mental: Mind is in the body, and is there where the body is at the moment. The group of states of consciousness corresponding to mind has accordingly the same location.

c) "Temporalisation" of the mental: Pure consciousness is at the same time its own "time field" *(eigenes Zeitfeld)* – a field of "phenomenological time", not of objective time. Objective time – one that represents itself in the process of physical perception –

---

[11] Vide *Ideen* II, § 49.

is, of course, brought in a point to point agreement with that time which is immanent in the stream of consciousness. Consequently, the states of consciousness appear to adjust themselves to the measurable time-structure of the physical nature. In that sense the "temporalisation" of mind would correspond to its localisation.

Following this method of reflection in phenomenological investigation, we come upon a further distinction between what are called "naturalistic" *(naturalistisch)* and "natural" *(natürlich)* attitudes. The former concerns men and human minds as belonging to nature; the latter stands for the "personalistic" attitude of the so-called moral sciences – an attitude which is characterized as "natural" in opposition to "artificial". Human mind, so far as it takes the position of "I", is transferred in naturalistic experience to the body which has physical appearance, and thereby assumes the local and temporal characterization of the latter. To that extent the situations connected with "I" belong to the real complex of physical (substantial-causal) nature; and in the latter the "empirical I" has its being and life.

Apart from this position of I, mind further combines in itself such acts as through which man becomes aware of the relation to his fellow-beings and of the real environment around him. In the naturalistic attitude, however, an objective physical totality of nature – as standing *out there* – is treated in abstraction from the said act relation. Consequently, we ourselves and all living beings become psycho-physical objects, and as such serve as possible themes for the relevant natural sciences. Personalistic attitude, on the contrary, implies that we human beings live with one another and are related to one another in various manners. Thus to live as a *person* is to posit oneself as a person, to place oneself in conscious relationship with the surrounding world *(Umwelt)*.

To speak in naturalistic terms, all consciousness functions in the *bodily* way, i.e., in the corporeal context. Understanding this situation of functioning in a naturalistic way, the totality of facts connected with personality would appear as *natural* data belonging to the domain of physical, or rather, psycho-physical nature. As such, the personal data form only a part of natural-psychological data. Thus, as Husserl points out, "from the standpoint of nature all that is personal is somewhat subordinated".[12] However, it should be made clear that these two points of view are not to be taken as equivalent, as on the same level. Indeed the personalistic attitude is to be given priority over the naturalistic, so far as the former marks the natural concrete way in which we come to be aware of ourselves and the world around us.[13]

III. *I-principle*

The principle around which the whole personal world is centred is that of I – "the I in the proper sense" *(das Ich im eigentlichen Sinne)*, as Husserl puts it.[14] Such I is necessarily to be conceived as active, so far as it is that which "posits an attitude" *(Stellungnehmende)*. It has its passive aspect too, for it accepts stimuli from things and reacts to them; but this "passive I" also is subjective in the original sense – similar as the "active I". In other words, the positing of attitude has its active as well as passive contexts or moments; but in both cases, "I" remains the subject of reference – or rather, the subject of intentionality. In the last analysis, the subject is essentially the subject of intentionality, and as such, it must be sharply distinguished from the given within the field of "subjective possession" *(subjektive Habe)*, to use the Husserlian expression – which in other words means subjective being, i.e., "being for the subject" *(Sein für das Subjekt)*.

So the I of intentionality is related in *cogito* to its surrounding world – to things and beings which it experiences. Subject has reference or relation to object, and the latter again stimulates the former. Subject can be in active or passive relation to object, which is present to the subject *noematically*, i.e., as the terminal point of reference. Thus in relation to the personal subject of intentionality, the object in the environment functions as object *for* it. This relation itself is, of course, not a *real* one but one of intentionality. Viewed from the side of object, it signifies that the noematic object *motivates* the subject, as it were, to tune itself with the object presented. Corresponding to the concept of

---

[12] ". . . vom Standpunkt der Natur ist alles Persönliche etwas Untergeordnetes", *Ideen* II, p. 185.
[13] Cf. L. Landgrebe, "Seinregionen und regionale Ontologien in Husserls Phänomenologie", *Studium Generale*, Juli 1956, p. 320.
[14] *Ideen* II, p. 213.

intentionality, the effect proceeding from the object to the subject is called by Husserl "motivation".

Thus the law of "motivation" operates in the personal-mental world, just as causality does in the natural-physical world. Again as the underlying functional principle of mental life in general, motivation can be viewed under different aspects – such as motivation of reason, association as motivation, motivation on the noetic side and on the noematic side. Be it in the context of the norm of reason, be it in that of mental associations and habit, or be it of the structure of consciousness in respect of thing-constitution in noetic and noematic aspects, motivation has in any case to be sharply distinguished from natural causality. As Husserl states the point: "The 'because-therefore' of motivation has a quite different meaning than causation in the natural sense".[15] Moreover, the unity of motivation can be spoken of with reference to "a correlation functionally grounded in the relevant acts themselves" (ein in den betreffenden Akten selbst fundierter Zusammenhang). And in this context alone should the causality of the personal (not natural) world and its relationship be interpreted.

In this connection it is further to be noted that the said motivation extends even beyond the actual sphere of just the individual. For the "empathy" (Einfühlung) into the consciousness of other persons enables us to comprehend the presence of motivation within the act spheres of other minds. The other person ("alter ego") is comprehended analogously to my own "I" as similarly a subject of a surrounding world of persons and things to which it relates itself in its acts. And the other person is also determined by the surrounding world which engulfs it; and thus the other person too is similarly subordinated to "law of motivation" (Gesetzlichkeit der Motivation).[16] In his "Cartesian Meditations" Husserl develops his theory of a phenomenological evidence of the experience of other persons. Such evidence is obtained through analogical apperception – as Husserl expresses it, "Appräsentation" – which is nothing else than a sort of mediate intentionality in respect of the experience of others.

---

[15] "Das 'Weil-So' der Motivation hat einen ganz anderen Sinn als Kausation im Sinne der Natur". Ibid., p. 229.
[16] Ibid.

IV. *Phenomenological analysis of person*

Two points of departure from which the phenomenological approach to the question of personality proceeds can be stated as follows.

A. Analysis of the phenomenon of personality – Regional constitution of person:

Proceeding as he does from the strictly phenomenological standpoint, Husserl does not come upon the metaphysical problem regarding the mode of being of person, nor does he posit person as substance. What primarily interests a phenomenologist is person as *phenomenon*, which appears as immanent within the region of pure consciousness. In the phenomenological order, the phenomenon of person belongs to the "region" of mind or spirit *(Geist)*.[17]

To be a person means in the first instance to be a subject of a world around us. So far as I am a person – and that applies naturally to every other person – I am inseparably bound with the world around me. Thus to each person belongs his world, and several communicating persons have at the same time a common world. This world around us is that of which personal I is conscious and to which it is related in different ways. The person in all its personal acts like representations, sensations etc., stands in relation to something, to an object in the world. To speak in general terms, this world around me is no world in itself, but one "for me" – i.e., the surrounding world of an I subject and experienced by him – intentionally given in experience. In this sense the world around us is never absolutely fixed, but it is in a certain sense ever in becoming.[18]

Here again the said motivation relation comes into forefront. Viewed in that light, the worldly relation holding among human beings as psycho-physical realities turns into a relation of personal subjects. In the light of the motivation relation between persons and things, both are not to be looked upon as existent in nature by themselves but as "intentional objectivities of personal consciousness" *(intentionale Gegenständlichkeiten des personalen Bewusst-*

---

[17] "Region" in the sense of phenomenologically constituted region, pertaining to different fields of experience. See above, p. 84; also Ch. VI, 3.

[18] *Ideen* II, § 50.

seins". Thus the effect of things in their bearing on consciousness is determined by the personal I. In a word, person acts as the centre of a surrounding world *(Mittelpunkt einer Umwelt)*.[19] Not only things but other subjects too are contained in the surrounding world. The subject thus views other subjects as persons who participate in their respective worlds around them. So long as a person is not considered in the context of the common inter-personal world around him, he is just theoretically treated – and only as a *thing*, but not considering his actual *personal* character.

B. The essence of person in the light of intentional act:

The phenomenological treatment of person is concerned not only with the phenomenon of personality as it is presented in reflection, but also with the deeper question regarding the essence of person in its subjectivity. The question here turns chiefly on the essence of person as subject of intentional acts. On the other hand, person as the centre of a surrounding world and as parti-cipating in the union of persons partakes of the character of the real-natural dimension too. The living embodied subject is so both with reference to the world around him and to his actual life at the same time. The guiding interest of phenomenological investigation, however, is directed to the aspect of person qua subject; for phenomenology, after all, is a philosophy from the standpoint of subjectivity. So far as the personal reality involved in the natural complex is essentially subjective, the question as to the essence of personality is, on the last analysis, determined by the genuinely phenomenological character of subject and his function.

Now, in the context of intentional act alone does the phenome-nologist speak of subject, i.e., the latter becomes phenom-enologically relevant. The phenomenological interpretation of objects proceeds in terms of intentionality, which again is to be understood ultimately with reference to the underlying principle of transcendental subjectivity. The latter, however, is essen-tially self-positing subjectivity, and as such assumes the form of "I am". This "I am", Husserl would agree, proves to be the phenomenological residuum, pointing to transcendental subjec-tivity as absolute. Yet this underlying self-positing subjectivity

[19] *Ibid.*

has to be comprehended, if in any way, only in the I-mode of being *(Ich-Sein)* rather than as metaphysically absolute consciousness.

V. *Person and Transcendental Subject*

At this stage the question may well arise: how to find out a relation between the so-called transcendental subject and personal I – or to put it in another way, between the subject that is presupposed and the ego that is accepted as fact? How far can the alleged transcendental ego, the last point of reference in the process of phenomenological reduction, be identified with the concrete ego, the real man – the former as well as the latter being both denoted by the common term "ego"? Before we come to the problem of the relation between transcendental ego and actual *(faktisches)* ego, we should consider the question of the identity of transcendental subject and I as person *(Ich-Person)* – person being understood in the usual sense of I, the rational self-conscious individual.

Following the phenomenological definition, as we have seen, the concept of person implies the centre of all positing of attitudes. I – in the sense of specific personal I – serves as the pole that exercises specific acts of positing and also the pole that is affected. So far as this personal I is the I of positing attitudes, the personal world proves to be the result of the decisions of the subject, and not as simply being there.

Now the question: are personal I and transcendental subject two mutually exclusive and distinct principles? The distinction between the two is not one of essence, but it rather lies in the methodological approach itself. I as person, and as such belonging to the world of fellow-beings and having a world around, is in point of essence the same I as transcendental subject. It is the point of view concerned which separates the two kinds of approach to the self-same principle. On a purely phenomenological approach, I sets itself as "transcendental ego", as the final point of reference which, on further analysis, proves to be the absolute region of consciousness, the source of all meaning of being. But when the position of the same transcendental ego is sought to be determined from the point of view of fact or actuality – the position in terms of concrete man and his surrounding world – the same transcendental ego would assume the form of person. So considering from the side of actual person, so far as the latter consciously posits itself in positing attitudes, it is promoted, so to say, to the level of transcendental subject.

On the dimension of reflective consciousness or transcendental self-consciousness, the "mundane" (i.e., world-involved) person, which acts, motivates and refers to the world, turns out to be itself the so-called transcendental ego. But actually it is not a case of transformation of the one to the other, for the two are not existentially distinct entities. However involved in the world the person may be in its unreflective attitude, even in that it proves to be the centre of all positing of attitudes. And here lies the key to the transcendental egohood of person.

Thus I the person is given as the object of reflective self-apperception in the wake of the development of empirical perception of I. The stream of experience in pure consciousness is necessarily a process in which pure I assumes the apperceptive form of personal I. The question may, of course, arise if personal I constitutes itself only on ground of reflection on I. If that be the case, what then is the factor which organizes the pre-reflective state of the ego? The answer can well be met by reference to the concept of "association" – although that need not bring the phenomenological position to the level of associationistic psychology.

Considered apart from associative contexts, the I that is constituted in reflection points to another I, viz., one constituted not out of experience (qua associative apperception) but out of life itself. In the original phase I am not actually a unity formed through associative and active experience, but rather "the subject of my life" ("das Subjekt meines Lebens") – and the subject develops through living.[20] So in view of the capacity of the subject for self-objectification in apperception, a distinction may be drawn between "I, that I am" on the subject side and "I, that I am" as object. The latter is represented by me in the form of existent "I am", as "me". As such, person is constituted for the I which is conscious as self.

[20] *Ibid.*, p. 252.

Again, to view it otherwise, this I, so far as it indicates essence-wise a unity, can also be regarded as a system of "I can", as Husserl puts it. This capacity (of "I can") is not an empty one but a positive potentiality. Personal I originally constitutes itself not merely as determined through instincts but also as higher, auto-nomous, freely active and guided particularly by motives of reason. In relation to my "centripetal I-acts" – i.e., the acts of reason which are referred back to person as the subject of those acts – I have actually the consciousness of "I can". Husserl prefers to draw a distinction between human person (in the external sense of the term) and person as subject of the acts of reason *(Vernunftakte)*. The former is to be understood as the apperceptive unity we grasp in self-perception, and the apper-ceptive perception of others, while the latter is to be approached as the agent of motivations, of the free life of acts.

Further, viewing personal I in the context of development, the other moment of I besides that of the higher stage of *free* I, i.e., I of free acts, has also to be taken into consideration. The char-acter of this so-called "unfree I" is grounded in the passivity of sensuousness, i.e., natural dispositions etc. Thus the spiritual I – in the specific sense of the subject of autonomous acts – finds itself dependent on a "dark background", as Husserl expresses it, of natural dispositions. Here again we come upon the Husserlian distinction between spirit *(Geist)* and mind *(Seele)*. Spirit as the agent of attitudes and motivations of reason stands over against mind at the lower stage of sensibility – a stage which corresponds to the associational level of psychology. It is here to be noted at the same time that the mind of the lower sense level is one with the subject of attitude. Both form an unbroken empirical unity, from which the unity of personal I that takes up an attitude stands as distinct. Regarding the position of mind in this connection, Husserl remarks, "It belongs to person presupposed as the functioning underground". *("Sie gehört zur Person als fundierender Untergrund")*.[21]

----

[21] *Ibid.*, p. 280.

VI. *Further Problem of Identity*

The further question as to how the pure transcendental I of phenomenology can actually be connected to person calls for a survey of the whole position regarding human-personal reality. The phenomenology of personality has its point of departure in what Husserl significantly calls "I-man" *(Ich-Mensch)*, which indicates – as the common term "I" ordinarily conveys – the total man with body and mind. As to the relation with body and mind in the context of this concrete I, the distinction that is to be taken into consideration is between these two positions: "I *am* my body" and "I *have* my body". While the former proposition cannot be accepted, the latter can be. Similarly we may consider the two possible propositions with regard to mind, viz., "I *am* a (or my) mind" and "I *have* a mind". Here again the former statement is not expressly maintained in the ordinary case, while the latter is. Body and mind, again, are such components as mutually involve each other, and thus form the unity that is man – the unity of the concrete I (one that Husserl prefers to designate also as *Geist)*.[22] Of course, in this unity the mental has a priority over the bodily, the former being the "expression of spirit" *(Ausdruck des Geistes)* as well as its "organ".

However, the actual I, i.e., the empirical psycho-physical complex of I that is man, does not provide for phenomenology its central point of reference. Rather the concept of subject as "pure I" is one that is phenomenologically significant. In conceiving subject necessarily under the basic form of "I", Husserl adopts and further extends the Cartesian conception of subject. Accordingly the whole formulation of the problematic concerning human being proceeds under this I-form. And this concept of I, again, so far as it encompasses the real man, would lead back correspondingly to the *pure I* in the background – one that Husserl sometimes designates as "pure mental I" *(rein seelisches Ich)*.[23]

[22] Cf. "Geist ist nicht ein abstraktes Ich der stellungnehmenden Akte, sondern er ist die *volle* Persönlichkeit, *Ich-Mensch*, der ich Stellung nehme, der ich denke, werte, handle, Werke vollbringe etc." – *Ideen II*, p. 280. So Husserl chooses the term "spirit" (if *Geist* could be so translated) to denote the totality of personal being, in which the empirical as well as the transcendental moments of personal life are united.

[23] Cf. Already in *Ideen I* Husserl holds that what remains as residuum after phenomenological "disconnecting" of the world and of empirical subjectivity belonging to that world is the pure I itself. (vide *Ideen I*, § 57). In *Ideen II* Husserl carries further

The possible approach to this so-called pure I would, of course, rest with such self-perception as may be obtained through abstraction from body. So abstracted and referred to the stream of experience as such, the supposed "I" should not be defined by the bodily locus. It is supposed to be that underlying principle in the life of consciousness which is directed to the perceived content in perception, to the known content in knowing, to the fancied in phantasy, to the thought content in logical thinking, to the valued in the act of valuing, to the willed object in willing. The pure I is thus to be conceived as the principle functioning in and through acts of mental life. As such, if at all to be distinguished from these acts, it could be so only in abstraction. [Of course, this should not mean that such pure I is to be taken simply as a nominal abstract concept – q. v. Ch. IV]. Indeed we come back to the point that subjectivity (and intersubjectivity) are to be posited presuppositionally behind empirical subjectivity (and intersubjectivity) - and as such, the two levels of I's and we's.[24]

In further clarifying the relation of human ego and pure I, it can be pointed out that former (i.e., I-man) is a constituent part of the real world around pure I *(Bestandstück der realen Umwelt des reinen Ich)*.[25] The latter exercises also such intentionality with which I the person constitutes itself. Every real I in this sense belongs to the "environment" *(Umgebung)*, so to say, of a pure I; the latter, so far as it apperceives in the form of "I, the man", has the human I or person for its object of environent. Thus correlative to man and human personality, pure I stands with its stream of consciousness. One may as well hold that there are as many pure I's as there are real I's. From the side of the real I it similarly holds good that it in a sense encloses the pure I in the manner of the essential content of apperception.

Viewing the problem from another side, a deeper antinomy is found to be involved in I-hood itself – I being subject *qua* non-object and object at the same time. Thus the "I" which becomes object in reflection seems evidently to be set over against that "I", which in its peculiar capacity as subject is in a position to

his investigation on pure I (sometimes referred to as "pure mental I" – but "mental" not in the empirical-psychological sense).

[24] Cf. "The 'I' and 'we' which we apprehend presuppose a hidden 'I' and 'we' to whom they are present." – Husserl, "Phenomenology" in *Encyclopaedia Britannica*.

[25] *Ideen II*, § 27.

make object of itself. Consequently a distinction between one "I" and the other has to be phenomenologically drawn.[26]

To put the point of distinction further in a typically phenomenological way, the *constituted* objectivity of personal "I" refers back to the *constituting* "I", which is itself not constituted. While personal I is present as an intentional unity constituted in relation to a possible infinite horizon, pure I lies numerically identical in all cogitos that are phenomenologically comprehensible. It is at the same time comprehended along with the act of reflection as functionally presupposed. Of course, even pure I in a sense belongs to personal I, so far as each act of cogito of personal I is at the same time the act of pure I too. The self-same act of cogito comes to be spoken of from two different levels – empirical and transcendental. What is otherwise held to be pure cogito, that is final subjectivity, turns through reflection into object and thereby relates to I-man – in other word, it is "personalised" *(personalisiert)*.[27] To be brief, in all these there seems to exist a reciprocal adjustment between pure or transcendental ego and personal ego, i.e., ego as ordinarily understood.

VII.   *Critique on Egology*

At this stage a further question – and an intriguing one – may well be posed concerning the basic phenomenological status of consciousness vis-a-vis ego – consequently, the question concerning the possibility of a "non-egological" interpretation of consciousness. Indeed the radical procedure of phenomenological reduction, if consistently followed, seems hardly to leave room for an I-principle, even if the latter be conceived in its purity. For consciousness, on ultimate analysis, proves to be only the "phenomenological residuum" – and the latter cannot evidently be expected to be intelligible with reference to the I-principle. Consequently one may rather prefer to speak of a "non-egological" structure of consciousness.

[26] In this connection a reference may be made to a different doctrine of Max Scheler: for him *I* in every sense of the word is still an object, while an act never becomes object; accordingly person in the living performance of act is never an object. Vide Scheler, *op. cit.*, p. 397.
[27] Vide Husserl, Ms. A VI 21.

It may be pointed out that there has been at least one such attempt at a non-egological interpretation – namely, by Aron Gurwitsch, himself a member of the Phenomenological movement. Phenomenological reduction, according to him, should leave transcendental consciousness strictly speaking only "as an apersonal or prepersonal field".[28]

In this connection the critique put forward by J-P Sartre on Husserl's theory of consciousness is particularly worth considering.[29] Sartre's contention is precisely that there is no ego "in" or "behind" consciousness; but there is only an ego *for* consciousness. For Sartre the ego need not be viewed in any special way; it is rather to be taken as "out there", "in the world" – as an object among objects. He contends that the ego is neither formally nor materially in consciousness; it is, on the contrary, "a being of the world, like the ego of another".[30]

In challenging the Husserlian egological position concerning the socalled transcendental ego or I, Sartre proposes to pursue the very principle of phenomenological reduction itself in all its consistency. Thus he begins by accepting the Husserlian contention that our psychic and psycho-physical *me* is a "transcendent" object, which should come under epoché in the same way as other objects do. But then Sartre raises the question direct: is not this psychic and psycho-physical *me* enough? Is there any need and justification for "doubling" it with a transcendental I, a structure of absolute consciousness?[31]

Behind Husserl's theory of "transcendental *I*" Sartre discovers a justification in the ordinary thought that consciousness has a need for unity and individuality. But the phenomenological conception of consciousness, Sartre observes, would render the unifying and individualizing role of such an *I* totally useless. On the contrary, the unity and personality of my *I* is itself made possible by consciousness. For, to be consistent in the phenomenological procedure, no exception can be made in the case of *I;* the *I*, in a strict phenomenological enquiry, proves to be as much

[28] Cf. A. Gurwitsch, "A non-egological conception of consciousness", in *Philosophy and Phenomenological Research*, I, 1941.

[29] Vide Jean-Paul Sartre, *The Transcendence of the Ego: An Existentialist Theory of Consciousness*, Noonday Press, New York.

[30] *Ibid.*, p. 31.

[31] *Ibid.*, p. 36.

a "relative existent" as the world itself – in brief, it is "an object *for* consciousness".[32] Thus Sartre sums up his contention: the transcendental *I* has no *raison d'être*.[33]

Now, in view of such a non-egological standpoint of the phenomenological existentialist, can there be a justification for the Husserlian theory of transcendental or pure ego? As earlier observed, Husserl refers to subjectivity essentially in the context of the ego – or rather the pure ego – as the identical subject-pole of the acts of consciousness, directing itself to objects. The pure ego, that exercises its pure functions of *cogito*, remains as the residuum through phenomenological suspension of the world, including empirical subjectivity.

Sartre's criticism of the Husserlian position seems to have ignored the sharply drawn distinction between the two levels of empirical psycho-physical I or ego and of the so-called transcendental subject. The *I*, which Sartre finds evidently reducible in wordly terms and as such "transcendent" (in the phenomenological sense), and consequently as amenable to "bracketing", has certainly been recognized in that way by Husserl. But for him such I only presupposes the other I, viz., pure ego. As Husserl unambiguously declares, "The 'I' and 'we' which we apprehend presuppose a hidden 'I' and 'we' to whom they are present".[34] And to ignore the distinction of the two levels to which they respectively pertain – in other words, to characterize the supposed transcendental I on the same plane as the ego as it is meant in ordinary use – would amount to a "category confusion".

However, Sartre's criticism serves as a warning against the Husserlian tendency of positing the pure I perhaps rather too easily. The expression "I" being used in common, how can one help attributing an egological interpretation to the phenomenological position of "transcendental subjectivity"? Perhaps the only justification in favour of the Husserlian position would be that consciousness, however "apersonal" it may be, has primarily to be conceived with reference to the subject in the form of "I". (Of course, such "I" may eventually take a purified or "rarefied" form – practically de-individualized). Further, if on Sartre's own

[32] *Ibid.*, p. 42.
[33] *Ibid.*, p. 40.
[34] Husserl's Article in *Encyclopaedia Britannica* (14th Ed.).

admission *I* is "more intimate" than *you* or *it* etc., then in point of phenomenological continuity it seems to be more appropriate to characterize the residuum – one that inescapably remains – in terms of "I" rather than any other category. Only it has to be scrupulously observed that such a deeper I is taken as "hidden" *(verborgen)*, as "anonymous".

VIII. *Final Paradox*

So we come back to the central problem of this essay, viz., of finding a bridge between the transcendental sphere of consciousness and the empirical sphere of human ego. We have to face the truism that transcendental consciousness belongs in reality to man – that is, it has a *concrete* situation in human existence. On the one hand, from the stratum of factual ego or person, the sphere of pure consciousness may well appear to be approachable; for even the former cannot be regarded as a mere thing among things, so far as it is characterized by the unique property of self-consciousness. (The point might again be urged against the Sartrean criticism mentioned above). From the side of pure consciousness, on the other hand, a concrete context or location – namely, in the shape of I-man *(Ich-Mensch)* – is called for.

Now, as a result of this review of the phenomenological treatment of personality, the paradox referred to in the beginning of this essay seems to reappear. It is the paradox, namely, of human subjectivity – *"Paradoxie der menschlichen Subjektivität"* – which means that the being, that is subject for the world *(Subjektsein für die Welt)*, is at the same time the being, that is object in the world *(Objektsein in der Welt)*.[35] This very truism of a coincidence in man of subjectivity in the form of object in the world and of subject in relation to the world – as Husserl expresses it, *"Subjektivität in der Welt als Objekt"* and *"für die Welt Bewusstseinsubjekt"* – poses for phenomenology a theoretical problem in itself. Towards meeting this problem, a similar question arises: how in man do the two aspects of subjectivity coincide – viz., as constituting the world, its meaning of being, and as

[35] Vide *Krisis*, § 53

determined by the world-order? To put the question in a different way: are transcendental subjects, which function constitutively for the world, men?[36] It may at once be pointed out that we, who are the subjects constituting meaning, are of course men in the natural-objective sense. For otherwise how could we at all be conceived as "we"? As men we are realities belonging to the world.

In attempting to resolve the said paradox, Husserl in all appearance separates and reunites at the same time the two methodological points of departure, viz., that of the mundane sphere as existentially posited and that of the transcendental subject. The one leads necessarily to the world; and for the other, the wordly givenness – including that of the person concerned – is nothing but "phenomenon". These standpoints cannot evidently agree in their exclusiveness of methodological approach. The consequence is an explicit division of the reality-status of the "mundane" I and of the being-status of the transcendental ego won through the performance of epoché. On ultimate analysis, the contrariety of the two attitudes has to be taken into consideration – the "natural objective attitude" of "common sense" and the attitude of the "uninterested observer" *(Einstellung des "uninteressierten Betrachters")*.[37] Similarly the opposition of the "pure" and the "empirical" in respect of the ego would correspond to the opposition between the "essencewise" *(wesensmässig)* and the "factual" definitions of being respectively.[38]

Now, taking all this into consideration, it seems to remain an open question for Husserl as to how it is possible for man, who is himself a thing of the world, to *constitute* at the same time the world and things.[39] On the one hand, the *I* finds itself within the world-horizon; it is *real* through its participation in the factual (spatio-temporal) world. On the other hand, within what empirically appears from outside as person, there lies subjectivity as the functioning-accomplishing ground. Through the latter

---

[36] *Ibid.*, § 54.

[37] *Ibid.*, p. 183. In this context Husserl also takes the factor of "transcendental intersubjectivity" (or "transcendental I of intersubjectivity") into consideration; for that too has to be constituted as man in the world. *Ibid.*, § 54.

[38] Cf. W. Biemel, "Husserls Encyclopaedia-Britannica Artikel und Heideggers Anmerkung dazu", *Tijdschrift voor Philosophie*, Mai 1950.

[39] *Ibid.*, p. 276 f.

alone can all objectivity – including the person himself – be treated as objective, related at the same time to subjectivity, i.e., as *phenomenon*. The latter again contains within itself the subject principle, the unique principle of transcendental activity – each man "carries in himself a transcendental I", as Husserl observes.[40]

This admission in phenomenology of the transcendental ego would not, however, as such lead further to a transcendence into the metaphysical ground of being. For Husserl chooses to remain on the level of essencewise definition of man – unlike in Heidegger's formulation of the problem of human being. On final phenomenological consideration, therefore, the transcendental ego would rather remain "anonymous" in relation to the factual ego.

[40] *Krisis*, p. 190.

CHAPTER VI

PHENOMENOLOGY AS PHILOSOPHY OF SCIENCE

I

A philosophical theory or doctrine can legitimately be expected to offer at least some philosophical exposition – even though implicit – of the rationale of natural science (or sciences). We refer here to a possible philosophy of science so far as it can be derived from Husserl's phenomenology. By that we mean something more definite and explicit than a bare reference to the basis of science as may be spoken of in connection with *any* philosophy. Phenomenology proposes a systematic analysis of experience in the first hand. In that respect phenomenology should generally offer some meeting-point with the positive sciences pertaining to special fields of natural facts and events. On the other hand, being itself a presuppositionless philosophy, phenomenology can hardly be expected to present a speculative theory of science – whether of the older "natural philosophy" type or of the so-called "synoptic" type of scientific philosophy.

However, the notion of science in general has never been distant from the Husserlian conception of philosophy. The original program of Husserl to build "philosophy as a rigorous science" stands as the guiding model of phenomenological philosophy as such, although its strength was subsequently lessened. In setting up this ideal for philosophy, Husserl evidently set his idea on the concept of *science (Wissenschaft)* in the broader sense, in a generalized sense. The Cartesian ideal of making an exact science of philosophy in line with mathematics never did leave Husserl in his philosophizing. The original sense of "science" in which it stands for exact knowledge and certainty is, for Husserl, guaranteed by the evidence of intuition.

It is to be noted, however, that although the image of "strict science" set the guiding notion of the Husserlian program, he was quite aware of the distinction in procedure between exact natural science and phenomenology. For phenomenology proceeds essentially by way of *describing*, whereas pure description can never be regarded as the *modus operandi* of positive sciences. Explanation and analysis, on the contrary, are the proper concern of science; and the scientific procedure, which necessarily involves the steps of abstraction, conceptualization, generalization and so on, departs from description.[1] Indeed considering the complete ideal of science, Husserl would not allow the bias of science to enter into phenomenological investigation. On the contrary, in a sense he even seems to prescribe "a rejection of science"[2] – in view of abstraction that science at its developed stage represents.

The distinction between natural and philosophical science has in fact quite sharply been drawn by Husserl. While natural sciences originate from the natural attitude of mind, philosophical science originates from the philosophical attitude. "Natural attitude" *(natürliche Denkhaltung)* is that in which mind turns to *things* in observation and thinking – to things which are given to us in a self-evident manner, even when the ways of being given and the kinds of being may differ. Natural knowledge grows by way of judgments relating to the world of perception. This is how the natural sciences of physical and psychical phenomena as well as those concerning mathematical entities like number etc. grow. Only in case of mathematical sciences, not only real objects are dealt with, but also the *ideal* ones or those valid in themselves.[3]

II

Indeed Husserl refuses to be carried away by the image of the so-called "modern science" or by the notion of "specialists" in science.[4] The method of science is determined, according to him,

[1] Husserl at one point draws a distinction between what he calls "descriptive" *(beschreibende)* and "explanatory" *(erklärende)* sciences, so far as concepts and theories are formed differently in the respective sciences. Vide *Ideen III.* p. 3f.

[2] Cf. M. Merleau-Ponty, *Phenomenology of Perception*, p. viii., trans. Colin Smith.

[3] Vide Husserl, *Die Idee der Phänomenologie*, I. *Vorlesung.*

[4] Cf. *Ideen III*, p. 22.

by the *a priori* of "phenomenological constitution", i.e., the essence of objects and of the possible experience of objectivity corresponding to the categories belonging to the respective spheres of experience. So far as the specialists are concerned, their task is to comprehend the particular problems and methods pertaining to different spheres of experience which correspond to respective fields of natural events and facts – and if required, to bring about philosophic formulations of concepts and norms.

So the method of all sciences, phenomenologically considered, has to be determined through the kind of originally given intuition which essentially belongs to the object category *(Gegenstandskategorie)*, to which it is related. All knowledge of nature is sought to be traced back to the final source in experience; all foundations of science rest finally on acts of experience – "acts" in the phenomenological sense of originally presenting objectivity to the reflecting mind. For in all science, the question of foundation would lead from the sphere of thought and construction to intuition, on ultimate analysis – i.e., to that which presents objectivity in the original moment of givenness. Thus to the different object categories should correspond the fundamental forms of originally presenting acts or the comprehensions, which in different ways constitute objectivities.[5]

Now the phenomenological study of science, broadly speaking, is concerned with the problem of correlating the theoretic superstructures of the natural sciences to the essencewise insight into the different regions of reality. In other words, the respective phenomenological sources corresponding to the different regions of reality are sought to be studied through the phenomenological method. Different sciences proceed with the bare presuppositions respectively of the different regions of reality – such as material thing, corporeal body, mind or ego etc. – each of which represents in broad a distinct objectivity to the reflecting mind. The science of "material nature", or the natural science of material things, provides for Husserl the starting-point – the science which takes nature as constituted in its unified spatio-temporal causal connections. According to the different stages in the constitution of material objectivity, along with the respective levels of meaning,

---

[5] *Ibid.*, p. 22f.

different stages of our knowledge of nature are determined. And the phenomenological investigation into the foundations of science is chiefly preoccupied with this matter.

III

In interpreting the method of science in terms of the intuitively given general essence of objectivity, we are inevitably led from the purely methodological question to that of the *ontological* basis of empirical sciences. As we have noted above, the method of science, when phenomenologically considered, has ultimately to be determined through original intuitions *(Anschauung)*. But there is another aspect of the method which is also to be taken into consideration, viz., the universal essence of objectivity itself. The essentialistic attitude is directed not merely to the comprehension of essence but also to the objective, which constitutes itself *(das sich konstituierende Gegenständliche)*. The general essence in view unfolds itself and thereby leads necessarily to an ontology. The perfect method of science presupposes the systematic formation of ontology, i.e., the theory of essence *(Wesenslehre)* which belongs to the respective object category.[6]

The exact question in philosophy of science that is to be dealt with at this stage is: how are the basic concepts and presuppositions of science to be analysed and interpreted? The position of Husserl on the issue of the genesis of concepts is *prima facie* empiricist. All concepts, whether general or particular, Husserl declares, originate from experience; and their usefulness is determined with reference to the continuance of further experience. But although Husserl admits that concepts grow out of experience through generalization, he does not thereby accept a conceptualistic position. For the meaning of general terms, phenomenologically considered, is to be interpreted as logical essences; and such meaning is taken to be valid only when logical thinking is not taken in its purely formalistic sense but as implying ideal possibility (see Ch. III). The latter again has to be

---

[6] A "theory of essence" *(Wesenslehre)* formed out of pure intuition is already anticipated in Husserl's investigations into the phenomenology of knowledge in *Logische Untersuchungen*. Vide *supra* Ch. III.

adapted to a corresponding intuition, comprehending the essence concerned – the corresponding "noema" which finds its true expression through the logical concept.

From the analysis of concepts it follows that they would be valid only so far as the possibility of a corresponding object were there. In the comprehension of the general essence it is presumed that the corresponding intuitive-noematic essence also is presented. But the noematic essence need not merely be presumed in meaning, but is also actually experienced in the originally presenting intuition. And in the latter case the "existential validity" *(Seinsgültigkeit)* of concepts is brought into effect, it is more than simple (or ideal) validity.[7] Husserl sharply distinguishes the pure meaning, which is free from all assertion, from the meaning which is charged with the *thetic* character, i.e., existential assertion. Thus even the concepts of higher generality are to be understood not merely in the light of bare noematic essence but also in terms of their real meaning. And this should hold good of all sciences in general, even the so-called "ideal" sciences.

IV

The specific business of phenomenology in interpreting the concepts and theories of science has to be further considered. Thus we come to one of the foremost tasks of phenomenology – namely, systematic investigation and scientific description of the cardinal divisions pertaining to the basic kinds *(Grundarten)* of essences as originally presented in consciousness. Each such fundamental kind corresponds to a *regional* concept, which encloses, and corresponds to, a *region* encompassing all objects to which this meaning is essentially relevant. The concept of "region" in phenomenological thought indicates an aggregate of objects in their homogeneous unity with respect to a particular natural science, corresponding to which a particular sphere of experience *constitutes* itself.[8]

A subtle distinction is drawn by Husserl in this connection

---

[7] *Ideen III*, p. 26.
[8] Cf. L. Landgrebe, "Seinsregionen und regionale Ontologien in Husserls Phäno-menologie", *Studium Generale*. Juli, 1956, p. 320. Also see Ch. V,

between "regional concepts" and "class concepts" *(Gattungs-begriffe)* – corresponding to the ideal and the existential validity of concepts respectively. Objective regional concepts are not derived through deduction from some postulates or out of certain system of *a priori* concepts not comprehensible in intuition – as Kant, for instance, intended in his "transcendental deduction of categories". Nor are they to be treated as class concepts employed in natural sciences, i.e., as generalizations from experience. So we have to bear in mind the sharp distinction in the formation of class concepts as in the light of phenomenological constitution of regions and as in the empirical sciences concerning different aspects of reality – *Realitätswissenschaften*. The difference between one class or kind and another – in all their respective degrees of generality – is obtained in one case through pure intuition of essences concerned, and in the other case through judicious consideration of the materials of experience. Objective regional concepts are thus in no way derivative but in essence originally comprehensible.[9]

Further, corresponding to regional concepts there is the *a priori* possibility of as many ontologies (i.e., "regional ontology"). For the *a priori*, represented in the form of *region*, is the source of possible ontologies *("Das Apriori im Sinne der Region ist der Quellpunkt der Ontologien")*.[10] The classification of natural sciences depends on the formation of regional concepts; therefore there should be different natural sciences corresponding to the different regional ontologies. Again the necessity and position of ontologies in different sciences and their peculiar role in the development of natural sciences are to be understood in the light of the original foundations of phenomenology. To take a broad instance of regional ontology as derived from the idea of regional constitution, the constitution of thing or material thing – *Dingkonstitution* – is a case in point. Thus material things in the outer world, with all their attributes and distinct relations, are sought to be brought under one "region" from the point of view of phenomenological constitution.

In this connection, the fundamental distinction between "experiential science" *(Erfahrungswissenschaft)* and "essentialistic

---

[9] Vide *Ideen III*, 97, p. 25ff.
[10] *Ibid.*, p. 36. Also see *infra*, Ch. VII. 4.

science" or eidetic science *(Wesenswissenschaft)* should be taken into consideration. While the former has existence *(Dasein)* in view, the latter pertains to essence *(Wesen)* – the essences which constitute the respective contents of possible existents generally in respect of different spheres. And eidetic science should in general precede experiential science, so far as the structure of possible essences precede, from the phenomenological point of view – i.e., from the point of view of "origination" – the stratum of facts.

Between facts and essences or eidetic concepts, again, another level, viz., that of universal regularities observed among empirical facts, can be pointed out. This level would come under theoretic scientific investigation, which would neither amount to an eidetic investigation nor could simply be reduced to the level of empirical investigations. Husserl further contends that theoretic scientific enquiry does not presuppose the eidetic; on the contrary, the former can direct itself to what is observed in experience, ascertaining order in it.[11]

V

The rationale of empirical generalization – obtaining general experiential judgments – has indeed been a recurrent theme in Husserl's philosophy. He takes up the problematic of probability *(Wahrscheinlichkeit)* directly from Hume, who traces the empirical judgments of probability – and general experiential statements cannot but be *probable* according to Hume – to psychological habits and associations. Husserl accounts for the Humean predicament concerning induction and probability by pointing out the exclusively *psychological* character of Humean analysis. The objective validity of laws, Husserl urges, cannot be derived merely from empirical generalization; rather it rests ultimately on the ideal possibility of an adequate consciousness of universals – or "general evidence" as Husserl would put it. Accordingly the ideal possibility of verification of the general empirical statements can be guaranteed through such evidence of generality in consciousness.[12]

[11] To take Husserl's illustration on this point, there had been an art of field-measurement (having purely an empirical basis) prior to the science of Geometry, which is a theoretic science; also there was an empirical science of astronomical observations before mathematical mechanics.

[12] Vide Husserl, *Erfahrung und Urteil*, Beilage II, p. 472ff. Also see Ch. II of this book.

The possibility of certain evidence of generalities in the form of essence-intuition seems in fact to bring the phenomenological position quite close to the Kantian system of pure reason. For in the former, as in the latter, the general truths and laws of science seem to be exempt from the predicament of probability, so far as they are grounded in the structure of thought itself (in phenomenology it is "purified experience" rather than "pure reason"). And here exactly the modern philosophy of science may step in with its method of "the analysis of actual scientific knowledge rather than the analysis of reason", as Reichenbach points out.[13] Even though recognizing the importance of a critique of knowledge, Reichenbach keenly criticizes the Kantian type of philosophizing through analysis of pure reason as incapable of yielding an adequate philosophy of science. Therefore, he suggests, a scientific philosophy of nature should not be concerned merely with analysing the potentialities of thought, but rather with analysing the products of thought and how it crystallizes in the form of elaborate scientific theories.[14]

So the question may be raised as to the legitimacy of a phenomenological analysis, proceeding as it does, on the basis of evidence and holding out a system of essences. Although largely sharing the Kantian critique of experience, phenomenology offers one salient point of distinction – in point of methodology and resulting thesis as well. Unlike the Kantian system, phenomenology does not seek to set up a fixed system of categories; rather phenomenology avowedly stands for an open system. And the latter is sought to be developed not as prompted by fixed categorization in thinking – here is the difference between phenomenological analysis and the Kantian "transcendental deduction of categories" from the logical forms of judgment, in keeping with the traditional scheme of categories.[15] In the phenomenological analysis, on the other hand, categories (i.e., essences) are posited as ideal preconditions of experience, obtained through the process of reduction carried on within different spheres and levels of experience.

In modern philosophy of science there is no scope for general

[13] Hans Reichenbach, *Modern Philosophy of Science*, Ch. IV, p. 79.
[14] *Ibid.*, p. 82.
[15] Vide *Ideen III*, p. 25.

presuppositions of knowledge; there are only presuppositions of particular hypotheses pertaining to and explaining the respective specialized fields of experience. Every scientific system has its own set of presuppositions; but it would be a futile attempt of the human intellect to seek for a universal set of presuppositions which should hold good of all possible systems of experience. So far as phenomenology is concerned, it does not propose a fixed universal scheme of postulates and presuppositions to which specialized fields of experience should fit in. The one major occasion – perhaps the only one – for such an intellectual fixation on the part of phenomenology appears when the latter comes to assert the one foundational principle of world-accomplishing subjectivity.[16]

So we have to take into consideration the demand of a progressive philosophy of nature to adjust its basic concepts or categories to the expanding range of specialized experience. Phenomenology, in its strict program and method, does not seem to come in conflict with such a demand. As to the rationale of scientific explanation in general, that there should be "close connection between content and form in actual science", as Reichenbach contends,[17] it may generally be pointed out that the "transcendental logic" proposed by Husserl aims exactly at a proper harmony between form and content of experience, as we have noted before (see Ch. III). In this connection comes into view the bearing that scientific research in different fields of knowledge has upon phenomenological investigations. What Reichenbach refers to as "autonomy of problems" operates as basic to science and theory of knowledge. Now the question arises: does phenomenological analysis of experience leave room for such "autonomy of problems"? In this regard the typical concepts of "region" and "regional ontology" may well provide a clue, so far as the concepts represent specialized fields of experience corresponding to different natural sciences (see above).

[16] The point is discussed in Ch. IV and Ch. VII.
[17] Reichenbach, p. 81.

VI

The actual ontological implications of the concept of "region" in the phenomenological analysis of scientific theories and concepts have further to be examined. The phenomenological method of intuitive analysis of essence serves at the same time to set out the categories of reality *(Realitätskategorien)* which are grounded in one another – such as, broadly speaking, those of matter, corporeal body, mind and "mental I", and so on. So far as the respective essences of these categories are derived from the sources of intuition, the original meaning of the corresponding regions of science *(Wissenschaftsgebiete)* is determined through them.

At this stage the ontological question in connection with the laws or theories of science should be closely considered, in view of the phenomenologist's contention regarding the ontological regions of objectivities connected to different systems of experience. For a scientific system of laws and facts is correlative to a system of ontology – and the interpretation of the former is necessarily accompanied by that of the latter. Within this area of problems the claim of a "physicalistic" interpretation would naturally come up for consideration. Quine refers to the advantage of a *physicalistic* conceptual scheme by virtue of "the rule of simplicity" in explaining the relation between sense data and objects. But Quine also points to two competing conceptual schemes, viz., the phenomenalistic and the physicalistic one. And he further seeks to reconcile the two by urging that the former is *epistemologically* more fundamental, while the latter is physically so.[18]

On further analysis, Quine points out that a transition from the phenomenalistic to the physicalistic point of view and from the latter, again, to the platonistic ontology – all these exhibit nothing but a movement from one level of "myths" to another. As he points out, from a phenomenalistic point of view the conceptual scheme of physical objects as approved in physicalism would prove to be a "convenient myth". From the point of view of a strictly physicalistic conceptual scheme, a platonistic ontology

---

[18] W. V. O. Quine, *From a Logical Point of View*, Ch. I.

concerning classes or attributes of physical objects would be no less a myth. Only this "higher myth" of ontology, Quine would admit, is "a good and useful one", so far as it simplifies our account of physics.[19]

Now such an approach to scientific theory would indeed be in tune with the attitude of formalism, as Quine himself admits. But what, after all, would be the outcome of such an approach? Would it not invite in the long run some sort of "fictionalism" in the field of scientific explanation? For the latter not only becomes devoid of all ontological efficacy, but theories of science concerning the physical world would prove to be nothing better than "ad hoc devices". If phenomenalism is to be accepted as the epistemologically satisfying theory – as Quine and Carnap would urge – then the ontologies of physical objects and mathematical objects would be reduced to sheer myths. Consequently, a gap between the epistemological and the ontological would ever remain in the area of scientific theory – and the priority of the epistemological would leave no room for the ontological.

It is in this context that the phenomenological attitude and method can offer a more satisfactory approach by combining – not externally but from within its very nature and methodology – the two points of view, the epistemological and the ontological. On the one hand, phenomenology would not give a free hand to epistemology so as to take on formalistic proportions on phenomenalistic lines. Nor, on the other hand, a theory of reality is asserted on the level of transcendent being. It is neither a question of manipulating possible hypotheses nor a question of deriving systems of experience from unconditioned realities. In no case does phenomenology offer a deductive procedure – neither in a purely formal way nor in ontological direction, i.e., in terms of the real. As Husserl declares: "Phenomenology is an infinite field of essence-analyses and essence-descriptions but not a field of deductions".[20]

---

[19] *Ibid.*
[20] "Die Phänomenologie ist ein unendliches Feld von Wesenanalysen und Wesenbeschreibungen, aber kein Feld von Deduktionen", *Ideen III*, p. 59.

VII

The crux of phenomenological-transcendental analysis of scientific knowledge lies in the relation of scientific theory and concepts to experience. In the rigorous scrutiny of phenomenology, different natural sciences, with their theories for explaining natural facts, prove to be untrue to experience. And the point to which phenomenology refers back again and again is the world of prescientific experience itself – *Lebenswelt*, as Husserl calls it. The scheme of knowledge which a science presents in its developed stage of theorization is found, on closer analysis, to embody only "an abstract and derivative sign-language", as Merleau-Ponty expresses it in respect of the stratum of prescientific experience.[21]

This brings us to Husserl's critique of modern science in general and the possible philosophical orientation arising therefrom. Husserl envisages a fundamental problem – a "crisis" indeed – in the widening gap between the prescientific world of experience and that of science produced through elaborate theoretico-mathematical framework. Husserl questions the very manner in which modern science poses its task and prosecutes its method. And he speaks of a "crisis", judging science (rather modern "science") not from within but in the light of the total situation of human knowledge, and taking a broad historico-teleological perspective of the development of scientific thought.[22]

In determining the development of *modern* science, Husserl takes Galileo as the turning point. The dominant feature in the transformation of the scientific-cum-philosophical view of reality as introduced by Galileo has cryptically been stated by Husserl as "mathematization of nature" *(Mathematisierung der Natur)*. The whole theoretic superstructure of physical science was presented within the framework of mathematics – in the language of mathematics. The guiding notion in the Galilean physics was the conception of Nature as "mathematical universe".

---

[21] Merleau-Ponty, *op. cit.*, p. ix.

[22] Vide Husserl, *Die Krisis*. In Part I and Part II of this last major work, Husserl expounds the so-called "crisis" of science, which he views as an "expression of the deeper crisis in the life of European man". The reader may also see A. Gurwitsch's article, "The Last Work of Edmund Husserl" in *Philosophy and Phenomenological Research*, 1956, pp. 380–99.

And the first step towards organizing his physics was that of *abstraction*. From the formal-mathematical representation of physical events and their regularities, the contents of sensuous experience were sought to be gradually eliminated or abstracted out. The Galilean formulations regarding the *possible* body in motion were in fact more an appeal to abstract conception than to actual perception of physical events. Through the method of abstraction alone could it be shown that an infinity of objects, which are otherwise relative to subjective experience and perception, can be determined in *objective* terms within the framework of an *a priori* method.[23]

As a result of mathematization and abstraction the world of common experience is relegated to the background – to a scientifically insignificant status of subjective appearance. An inevitable gulf arises between the Nature of the physicist, read in mathematical terms, and Nature as actually experienced. This divorce between the physicist's view of the universe and the primary world of experience remains the dominant problematic feature throughout the course of modern physical science succeeding Galileo and Newton.

In analysing further the impact of mathematization, Husserl points out – rather metaphorically – how the common world of our unsophisticated acceptance is sought to be interpreted in terms of "garment of ideas" *(Ideenkleid)* – the garment of symbols – which might fit in the indefinite range of possible experience.[24] The framework within which the so-called objective scientific truths operate is that of *symbols* – and in terms of the latter the totality of things originally present in the *Lebenswelt* can possibly be represented. The so-called "garment of ideas" obscures our understanding to the extent that a distinction between what is methodological and what is ontological is missed; the framework of symbols, after all, serves as the means for interpreting the physical world and is not itself the being of this physical nature. The meaning of method *qua* method is thereby lost sight of.

The philosophical impact of the Galilean "new science" may

---

[23] Besides Galileo's mathematical theory of motion, Descartes' greatest scientific invention, i.e., analytical Geometry and Newton's *Principia Mathematica* – all displayed in some way or other the said method of abstraction.

[24] Cf. *Die Krisis*, p. 53ff.

in one word be characterized as "objectivism". And his objectivism, developed in the philosophy of physicalistic rationalism, was further founded on the rational model of natural-scientific method; the latter yields the conception of nature as a closed and self-contained material system, in which all spatio-temporal events are determined. The "meaning of being" *(Seinssinn)* that pertains to the world presented at the level of common experience, can in a sense be regarded as a *subjective* product, so far as the meaning and significance of such a world is constituted through the prescientific level of experience. The so-called *objective* truths concerning the world of science are, on the other hand, to be regarded as products of abstraction at the higher stage of reflection, having pre-scientific thinking and experience as their ground.

Now, Husserl's aim has been to show the link between the alleged objective *a priori* of science and the admittedly *subjective* level of *Lebenswelt*. And the connecting link sought for seems to be provided by that fundamental principle of subjectivity which constitutes not only the meaning of being of the prescientific world of immediate experience but also of the full-fledged scientific picture of the universe. For on the one hand, even the naïve subjective world accepted in our unsophisticated attitude, if analysed, appears to exhibit apriorities of some sort – what Husserl calls *"lebensweltliches Apriori"*.[25] (Thus he refers to the evident uniformities and regularities that can naïvely be grasped in prescientific experience – such as, causality, without having its fuller scientific import.) On the other hand, the concepts of objectivity, if analysed essentialistically, reveal the meaning-constituting subjectivity.

That guarantees the possibility of a link between what is generally accepted in science as the objective *a priori* and what may be regarded as the apriorities pertaining to prescientific experience. The way to render objective scientific truth intelligible lies in falling back radically – as the problematic of *Rückfrage* denotes – upon the final precondition that is subjectivity, in which all validity of meaning is ultimately grounded. And that would, of course, mean a rejection of what is accepted as the obviously objective being of the world. Instead subjectivity

---

[25] Vide *Krisis*, 36. Further see on *Lebenswelt*, p. 128.

should be regarded as the final precondition both in respect of the naïve presentation of prescientific experience as well as of the rationalized objectification of that stratum of experience.

VIII

Thus phenomenology not only offers a critique of the fundamental method and outlook of modern science, but also seeks to reconstruct the very foundations of scientific knowledge. The fundamental critique of Husserl against science is that of *objectivism*. And the latter means a serious fault, because it can be achieved only through completely losing sight of the original foundations of meaning *(Sinnesfundament)* upon which the superstructure of scientific knowledge is built. For the knowledge of every natural science is originally based on the evidences obtained from *Lebenswelt*, and by virtue of that rootedness in the original evidences *(Ursprungsevidenzen)* alone could natural sciences bear their constant meaningfulness for the world and for life – *Lebensbedeutsamkeit*, as Husserl says.

Consequently the remedy that Husserl prescribes for meeting the said "crisis" is restoring the link with the prescientific world of common experience, the original home of all regularities that eventually find place in the theoretic superstructure of natural science. In order to assess the precise meaning of the picture yielded by the mathematico-theoretical framework of science, we have to render that "translatable" (to borrow the analyst's expression) in terms of the basic experience of prescientific world. On the level of theory, science may thus be regarded as "the second-order expression", as Merleau-Ponty points out.[26]

A possible objection may be raised on the Husserlian formulation of "crisis" from the point of view of "operationalism", according to which a scientific concept is treated as synonymous with the corresponding set of operations. Scientific concepts and theories, if interpreted in the operational context, need not as such imply a "crisis" in the Husserlian sense. Instrumentalistic, operationalistic and positivitics interpretations of scientific theories

---

[26] Merleau-Ponty, *op. cit.*, p. viii.

all agree on the point that theoretical concepts are purely computational devices – or "logical constructions", as sometimes held – whose only function is to make the prediction of observable facts easily possible. We need not here enter upon the controversial issue in modern philosophy of science over the definition of the theoretic concepts of science – the controversy chiefly between the two schools of interpretation, viz., positivistic and realistic. For the present discourse we have to recognize the significance of operationalism so far as it stresses the importance of operations in the definition of concepts. But it tends to stress exclusively the operational aspect in determining the meaning of a concept and to neglect the essential content on which the operation is performed.

Moreover, a purely positivistic-operationalistic account presents no doubt a logical analysis of the structure and the empirical basis of scientific theories; but it does not provide an account of the origin or development of theories. At this point the unique approach of the phenomenological problematic can be appreciated. Instead of confining itself to the level of operational definition with reference to the so-called observable facts, phenomenology rather proceeds to the higher-order problem of genetic analysis – *Ursprungsproblem.*

At this stage a lingering doubt may still be put forth: does not phenomenology, in positing its problem and formulating its approach, tend to be essentially indifferent – if not antagonistic – to natural science? Confined strictly to its own method of reduction, phenomenology is apt to turn essentially anti-scientific – in the sense of "anti-naturalistic", as Marvin Farber, for instance, has pointed out.[27] One may hesitate to accept the phenomenologist's attempt at reducing regularities of nature to nonfactual essentialities as natural-scientific. To be true to the verdict of natural science, its method and outlook, the laws of nature which science proceeds to discover should be treated as valid for the world of facts.[28]

---

[27] Cf. M. Farber, "Experience and Transcendence", *Philosophy and Phenomenological Research*, Sept. '51; also, *The Foundation of Phenomenology: Edmund Husserl and the Quest for a Rigorous Science of Philosophy*, p. 535.
[28] Cf. Moritz Geiger in *Proceedings of the Sixth International Congress of Philosophy* (1926): ". . . the arguments taken from the reality of laws of nature not only maintain that essences are given but also that they are real", p. 276f.

As to this charge of being anti-scientific, it may at once be pointed out that phenomenology admittedly does not offer to be a natural science itself – although it claims to be "scientific" in a more general sense of the term.[29] The minimum of metaphysical commitment that is usually associated with scientific theory and method is that of naturalism – or differently put, physicalism (noted earlier in this chapter). Now the phenomenological attitude as such need not be in conflict with the facts and events of nature determined by natural relations and conditions. But it would refuse to submit to a particular standpoint, i.e., the naturalist, which recognizes the natural being as the only real one.

What, then, may be the bearing of phenomenological explanation on a possible philosophy of science? It is clear that phenomenology as critique of experience is not concerned with the problem of ordering facts in the shape of laws of nature. It rather takes upon itself, as we have already noted, the higher-order problem of analysing the epistemological (or rather, transcendental) preconditions of scientific knowledge. And that sets the priority of the "epistemological point of view" – one that Quine admits to be connected with the phenomenalistic point of view.[30] But phenomenalism, as we have considered (Section 6), only leads to fictionalism – the predicament to which modern science at large, in its developed theoretic phase, is subject, as a result of its ideal constructions. All this brings into particular relief the significance of the Husserlian prescription of a trace-back to the basic stratum of experience in common life.

---

[29] Reference to "*Philosophie als strenge Wissenschaft*".
[30] Quine, *op. cit.*, p. 19.

CHAPTER VII

IS PHENOMENOLOGY
ONTOLOGICALLY COMMITTED?

I

The question whether a philosophy is ontologically committed or not may in the first instance appear to be either superfluous or trivial. From a point of view, according to which a philosophical theory worth the name has necessarily to posit the nature of being as it really is, the question would prove to be redundant. If the business of philosophy is, on the other hand, taken to be conceptual clarification alone, it would turn to be a trivial question whether a philosophy holds to a final view on the nature of what there is. However, the question has to be accepted as a real one when two conditions are taken into consideration – either one or both of them. (a) In one case an ontological commitment would constitute an essential part of the philosophical position concerned, though not explicitly formulated as one. (b) In another case a philosophical position would imply a reference to an ontological standpoint arising as a logical demand to fulfil the philosophical inadequacy involved in the idea of a purely deontological interpretation of experience.

Both these aspects of the question would come into play in understanding Husserl's phenomenology. And the question comes out perhaps all the more sharply in phenomenology, just because the latter professes to be a philosophical discipline free from metaphyscial presuppositions. Husserl proposes his program for a presuppositionless radical philosophy which should itself shape into a "rigorous science".[1] Negatively speaking, the alleged "scientific" character of the new discipline pertains to its

---

[1] Cf. "Philosophie als strenge Wissenschaft", Husserl's article in *Logos*, 1910–11.

freedom from any theorizing concerning the so-called ultimate nature of reality. On the positive side, the procedure should be on the sure foundation of "evidence", of that which alone can impart *certainty* to knowledge. Consequently, a science of the preconditions that make experience and knowledge possible – in other words, "a science of the evident in consciousness", as phenomenology, sharply distinguished from psychology, is sought to be defined – would hardly involve a theory concerning "being as being".

Ontology seeks for the final meaning of existence – of what there *is* on ultimate analysis. To be ontologically committed would thus mean to adopt a definite view concerning the ultimate mode of being or existence – a view which, if adopted, should orientate the explanation of experience as a whole. Whether obtained through speculative reasoning or intuited as self-evident, the position regarding being presents to the philosopher concerned an intellectual obligation, so to say, to interpret every facet of reality in terms of that principle – and not a mere hypothetical possibility. So far as traditional metaphysics goes, ontology in some form or other constitutes the central part of philosophical enquiry. This would follow from the alleged nature of metaphysics itself, which basically involves an insight into the ground of things as providing the key to all significant philosophical questions.

II

Phenomenology, offering to be a self-complete discipline, proposes a metaphysically non-committal attitude. That as such need not mean that phenomenology is anti-metaphysical, fighting the very possibility of an alleged science of the supersensible reality. Rather it prefers to shift its interest – almost deliberately so – from metaphysical questions to an analysis of experience. It seeks accordingly to shelve all presuppositions concerning the nature of the real – be it on the ordinary *factual* level or be it on the so-called *higher* level of unconditioned being. Consequently it proposes to depart from a commitment to a belief either in the factual reality of common acceptance or in the transcendent reality of "First Principles". In other words, neither a naturalistic nor a metaphysical commitment should come in the way of the phenomenologist's programme for a "First philosophy" *("Erste Philosophie")*.

However, the outright denial of either the existent fact or of the so-called "first principles" is not as such involved in the program itself. An expression which Husserl uses in this regard explains the typically non-committal attitude of his, viz., "brackcting". i.e., suspending belief in the question of reality, whatever may be the object under reference. The doubt may, of course, occur if this attitude of indifference did not, in its consistency, virtually amount to one of denial – at least so far as the higher reality is concerned. To this question we shall turn subsequently in our discourse.

Phenomenology poses primarily a *methodological* program. It is to be understood more as a line of analysis than as a system of truths regarding the nature and categories of reality. And methodologically, again, it offers to be thoroughly non-committal so far as metaphysical questions are concerned. As a mode of analysis of experience which is neither to be psychological nor natural-scientific, phenomenology seeks to proceed with reference to meaning-essences. And the latter are to be understood not as essences of the real but rather as *immanent* within what Husserl calls "the region of purified experience". That would mean, all transcendences beyond the region of immanent consciousness are to be dismissed; and the essential constitution of consciousness lies in "intentionality" or referential character.

The confinement of the subject-matter of phenomenological investigation within the region of immanent consciousness (which is essentially "intentional") and the rejection of the transcendent may have an immediate bearing on the question of ontological commitment. This insistence on apodictic evidence in consciousness as yielding the foundation of philosophical science would *prima facie* exempt phenomenology from the charge of meaninglessness. The latter charge is brought from the standpoint of logical analysis against a body of knowledge that pretends to reach above or behind experience – as positivists like Carnap or Ayer would argue. As a matter of fact Husserl prescribes what he calls "epoché" – or rather, "transcendental epoché" – not merely towards the common-sense belief in existent facts and natural laws of science but also towards metaphysics itself. What he means is *a disconnecting* of the natural belief in the existent real as the ideal precondition for obtaining the pure phenomenological region of consciousness. And this attitude of suspense towards the question of being is evidently extended at all possible levels of ontology.

However, regarding the methodological insistence on immanence in experience and evidence in consciousness, further clarifications are required. What Husserl means by experience – or rather, the region of *purified* experience – should not in any way be understood from a *psychological* point of view. "Experience" is not to be taken in the sense of mental factuality, corresponding to which physical facts can be discovered. Husserl takes pains to distinguish phenomenology sharply from psychology, the latter necessarily being a natural science of the mental. The objects of phenomenological investigation are not the actual contents of mind – what actually goes on in the mind – but the *ideal* objectivities to which consciousness is related by way of modes of referentiality. What is thus referred to as purified region of experience or consciousness does not indicate *mental* facts or ideas in the common psychological sense of the term. It rather means the "reality-neutral" seat of non-factual idealities – and all transcendences in knowledge are to be essence-wise "reduced" to the latter.

This brings us at once to the basic distinction between fact and essence in phenomenology. In characterizing the peculiar status of essences as distinguished from facts, Husserl prefers to treat the former as "irreal", i.e., what we may call reality-neutral. Of course, Husserl does refer to the "eidetic being" of the essences – irreal, non-psychological, non-natural as they are. And this admittedly is an *ontic* characterization, though it need not amount to an ontological one. The distinction between "ontic" and "ontological" should not be taken as a play upon words; it has a real significance. In opposing the *psychologistic* tendency of explaining the idealities away as entirely of psychological origin, Husserl urges their trans-mental character – even to the extent that they are brought on par with the Platonic "Eidos". But to recognize an element of *transcendence* about the essences need not be equivalent to the assertion of transcendent reals. For, after all, they hold good as conditions for the possibility of experience – and thus necessarily in the context of functional referentiality of consciousness, or as subjectively meant.

III

It is interesting to note how the expression "ontology" does occur in phenomenological philosophy – and in more than one context. How far such uses of "ontology" would go against the otherwise deontological viewpoint of phenomenology is also worth considering. To take the first instance, the notion of ontology occurs in the Husserlian philosophy of logic as the concept of "Formal Ontology". Already in Husserl's elucidation and critique of formal logic, it constitutes a distinct phase; corresponding to pure formal analytic dealing with the pure forms of predicative judgment, one may speak of formal ontology. For, as Husserl maintains, the analytic as the formal theory of science is at the same time "ontically directed and is *ontological* by virtue of its *a priori* generality". Thus formal logic in its primary movement is directed to judgments in general and takes on the shape of formal apophantic; and the same logic in another phase is directed to objectivity in general and thus assmues the shape of "formal ontology".

What is, however, to be noted in the Husserlian formulation of formal ontology is that it is not proposed as a distinct theory by itself, positing its own level of truths. Formal ontology has for itself a region over and above the logical region of propositional forms – its subject-matter being "the empty form of region in general". The transformation of the formal-apophantic logic to a formal ontology is obtained through a shift from what Husserl calls "apophantic attitude" to the "ontological". This admission of the possiblity of an ontological attitude proceeding from pure logic can at best be understood as a possible extension of the region of apophantic logic towards the ontic direction of object-in-general. But this need not be interpreted as *ontologizing* the logical forms, although a platonizing tendency in respect of logical and mathematical forms is quite marked in Husserl since his "Logical Investigations". In fact the so-called "formal ontology" marks only a theoretically *possible* intermediate stage in the elucidation of the true philosophical logic, i.e., "transcendental logic", as Husserl proposes to designate it.

Perhaps a more decisive use of the notion of ontology in the Husserlian system occurs in respect of the expression "regional ontology". Proceeding from the phenomenological outlook and method, Husserl develops the central theme of constructive phenomenology, viz., that of "phenomenological constitution" in respect of the different regions of being out of different spheres of experience. The problem of "constitution" seeks to extend the notion of "intentionality" to the forming of the object in consciousness as "phenomenon".[2] In terms of the constituting activity of consciousness, transcendental and non-psychological as it is, the structures of intended objectivities and the unity of meaning of the intended world are to be comprehended.[3]

Now, does the so-called regional ontology envisage a truly ontological scheme? If we are not misled by mere nomenclature, we should hardly lose sight of the concept as presumably differentiated from a genuinely metaphysical assertion. The point of view of constitution, nay of the whole of phenomenological investigation itself, is that of the conditions of the possibility of knowledge of objects rather than objects themselves or being in itself. As Husserl rather unambiguously puts the point, transcendental phenomenology is the phenomenology of constituting consciousness, and so no single objective axiom – those pertaining to objects which are not consciousness – belongs to it.[4]

It may further be noted in this connexion that this ambivalent notion of "regional ontology" in Husserlian philosophy was adopted in right earnest by Heidegger in respect of human existence *(Dasein)*. And taking the latter as actuality, the regional

---

[2] The second volume of Husserl's *Ideas (Ideen,* II) has for its theme "the phenomenological investigations into constitution" – the problem of "objective regions" and their "transcendental constitution".

[3] For further implications of the concept of "regional ontology" or "regional constitution" – particularly in the context of Husserlian philosophy of science – see chapter VI.

[4] "Die transzendentale Phänomenologie ist Phänomenologie des *konstituierenden Bewusstseins* und somit gehört kein einziges objektives Axiom ... in sie hinein ..." – quoted from Husserl's manuscript in Walter Biemel's Introduction to Husserl's *Die Idee der Phänomenologie* (Husserliana, Band II).

ontology concerning human subject met with a thoroughly ontological orientation in the shape of what Heidegger develops as his philosophy of existence *(Existenzphilosophie)*. What has been for Husserl a *theoretic* region in the analysis of experience is transformed in Heidegger's thought into the very key to the question of being. Thus the Husserlian region of "Spirit" *(Geist)* – under which the category of "person" is included – no longer indicates for Heidegger a mere theoretic possibility of a broad range of phenomenon evident in consciousness, but it provides the very index to the question of Being. (Indeed Husserl is too keenly aware of the possibility that transcendental phenomenology of consciousness may be verging on "anthropologism", centred round human reality.)

IV

Two issues may further be pointed out on which the question of ontological commitment seems to be almost unavoidable. One definite case where the question comes up quite relevantly is that of the status of "essences". Can essences possibly be conceived as devoid of reality? Now they could be real at either of the two levels – that of natural facts of experience or that of the alleged unconditioned being. Either essences are viewed as *naturalized* – as real *essences* of actual experience; or they are ontologized – as non-factual realities of a higher order. Phenomenology seeks to avoid committing itself at either of these two levels.

However, a doubt may arise if the so-called *ideal* objects, meant as essences, could at all be referred to except as "they *are* there". Now the meaningfulness of statements concerning the alleged essences, each taken as individual – as in the case of any singular term – need not presuppose an *entity* named by the term. As Quine puts it. "A singular term need not name to be significant".[5] Frege's analysis also has amply demonstrated how meaning and naming can differ, even in respect of a singular term which is genuinely a name of an object (Cf. the examples of "the morning star" and "the evening star" etc.).

[5] W. V. Quine, "On What there Is", *From a Logical Point of View*, Ch. I.

Turning to phenomenological essences, it can be said that they stand for pure *meanings* rather than *objects* which are named or meant. And in the latter case alone can one definitely speak in terms of "there is", but not in the former. So far as phenomenology makes for a critique of experience, it need not posit the ideal implicates of (or behind) experience either as facts or as super-facts. Its methodological viewpoint is not that of asserting phenomena in entitative terms but rather in terms of authentic evidence in the reflecting consciousness itself. Phenomenology proper, which is *epistemologically* oriented rather than psychologically, seeks to offer a doctrine of the essence of knowledge; and it can arise only when all empirical reference remains suspended.

Not only is empirical reference to be suspended. Husserl further holds the point quite unambiguously that transcendental phenomenology has nothing to do with *a priori* ontology, with "a priori real ontology of any kind".[6] Indeed the pure epistemological or "transcendental" interest does not lie with objective being and exhibition of truths concerning objective being. On the contrary, even the typical problem of "phenomenological constitution" – the central theme in the constructive phase of Husserlian philosophy – is concerned with the question how objects *constitute* themselves in consciousness, in respect of the different "objective regions" of experience. Thereby the notion of intentionality is sought to be extended to the sphere of the formation of objectivity in intending consciousness. As Husserl puts the essence of the problem, it is "the resolution of being in consciousness" (*"die Auflösung des Seins in Bewusstsein"*). The entire interest of transcendental phenomenology is turned on the constituting consciousness itself – or as Husserl simply puts it, "consciousness as consciousness". And what is sought to be emphasized here is that no single "objective axiom" – such as pertain to objects which are not consciousness – would be a part of constitutive phenomenology.[7]

But there may remain a further lingering doubt in this regard – and one that takes its hold on the foundation of the phenomenological standpoint itself. It is the question regarding the

---

[6] Vide Biemel's Introduction to *Die Idee der Phänomenologie*.
[7] *Ibid.*

nature and status of consciousness, otherwise termed "transcendental subjectivity". Husserl himself prefers reticence in respect of the ontological question on consciousness, and proposes a more non-committal expression, viz., "phenomenological residuum", in order to characterize consciousness. The latter is what would ideally remain after all phenomenological reductions have been performed, as the final stratum of reference, itself irreducible. How else could we speak of consciousness, consistently from a phenomenological point of view? For, after all, the point of view of "function" prevails as one central to the phenomenological enquiry.

Yet the question looms large again and again in the horizon of Husserl's phenomenology. Considering his descriptions of subjectivity as "autonomous region", as "accomplishing *(leistende)* subjectivity", and finally as the ground of world-meanings or world-constitutions, the question of the ontological status of consciousness seems hard to shelve altogether. Does not Husserl himself consider consciousness as the constituting ground of all meanings of being *(Seinssinn)?* It would then seem to be rather improbable that such a principle, referred to in this way, should itself be – except through a *tour de force* – divorced from being. As Thévenaz, a discerning exponent of phenomenology, remarks: in pushing the search for the radical and primary foundation of all knowledge towards a transcendental direction, Husserlian philosophy "requires a general theory of being, an ontology".[8]

V

That an ontological concern has been latent in phenomenological investigations can hardly be denied. Already in the earlier phase of philosophizing, in his critique of formal logic and elucidation of a philosophical logic, Husserl does make use of the expression "formal ontology".[9] Only the latter does not amount to any *ontologizing* of the logical forms, but first stands

---

[8] Pierre Thévenaz, *What Is Phenomenology?* (Quadrangle).

[9] Formal apophantic logic, when ontically directed to objectivity in general, takes on the form of "formal ontology". Vide Husserl, *Formale und Transzendentale Logik*. See above, Ch. III.

for a theoretically possible intermediate stage in proceeding from pure analytic to transcendental logic. Coming to the more definitive expression of "regional ontology", again, the notion of "ontology" is used purely from the point of view of constitution. And the latter admittedly pertains, on final analysis, to the conditions for the possibility of knowledge of objects rather than to objects themselves or being-in-itself. Thus both these uses of the expression "ontology" may be taken as somewhat exempt from genuinely metaphysical assertions.

However, as we come to the later phase of Husserl, the said ontological concern is found to be rather polarized – perhaps through an inner demand of consistency – in the direction of a new metaphysics, one that positively tends to take on an idealistic shape. In his "Cartesian Meditations" Husserl just stops short of claiming ontological status for consciousness, even departing from a purely egological view of the same. The implicit demand for ontological validity seems to be more pronounced in the last work of Husserl, viz., "The Crisis of European Sciences and Transcendental Phenomenology". In the latter, transcendental subjectivity is shown to be the ground of all world-constitutions.

In spite of all this ontological drive more or less implicit in phenomenology, the "being" which is in question is far from that of Scholastic or of Hegelian ontology. With its arrow-head no doubt set in the direction of an idealistic metaphysics of consciousness – be it of the Cartesian or of the Hegelian sort – phenomenology does stop short of an ontological consummation which might otherwise have been almost inevitable. The primary methodological aim of holding to the evident in the interpretation of the true, of relating transcendence to experience (the latter principally in the form of what Husserl calls "life-world"), has certainly gone a long way in suspending the final adoption of an ontological standpoint. Positively stated, the question of a metaphysical standpoint is finally kept as an *open* one. And that could be so, because unlike in a deductive system of speculative theory, phenomenology would not start from any premises about what is to be accepted as real; nor does it hunt for such premises in order to proceed deductively to a self-complete system of metaphysical truths. On the contrary, phenomenology would rather prefer the approach of "going over the ground, standing back and saying: look" – as Waismann puts it in explaining his idea of philosophy.[10]

VI

If exempt from the charge of dogmatic ontology in the traditional sense, phenomenology may still have to face a charge of dogmatism in respect of its method and program. Husserl set for his new discipline the goal of "absolute certainty" as the foundation of all knowledge, so that philosophy could turn on the sure path of exact science. This evidently reflects his mathematical bias in philosophizing – pre-eminently in line with Cartesianism. But this preliminary target, rather too ambitious as it seems to be, need not be mistaken for an attempt to model his philosophy on the axiomatic-deductive lines of rationalistic metaphysics. This should rather be understood as a methodological belief which can well be regarded as almost a working precondition in an inquiry into consciousness, knowledge and experience on new grounds free from presupposition. (Even Hume did believe in his new "experimental method" in an attempt to build a "science of human nature".)

This stress on the *methodological* context rather than on resulting position and theme marks many a cardinal concept in the phenomenological discipline. It may be particularly instructive in this connexion to draw a sharp distinction between two uses of cardinal concepts in a philosophical theory. To adopt a distinction aptly made by Eugen Fink, a close critic of Husserl's phenomenology, certain key concepts in a system are to be regarded as "operative", while others are "thematic".[11] Operative concepts are presupposed in thinking as the conceptual medium through which thought operates rather than asserted as a result of thinking. Instead of themselves being the themes in a philosophical thought, they rather act as the "operative shades" of thinking. We are directed to the themes through the medium of operative concepts.

In the phenomenological system (if at all it could be called a

<hr>

[10] F. Waismann, "How I see Philosophy", *Contemporary British Philosophy*, Third Series.

[11] Eugen Fink, "Operative Begriffe in Husserls Phänomenologie", *Zeitschrift für philosophische Forschung*, XI, 3. 1957.

system), the said operative concepts are to be met with in those of "phenomenon", "epoché", "constitution", "transcendental logic". As to all these concepts, we are apt to conceive them merely as *thematic*, i.e., as those in which thinking fixes itself. But as Fink remarks, they are more "operatively used rather than thematically classified", as such they all present problems which are still "open". In this sense, extending Fink's formulation a little further, we might say, the phenomenologist's reference to being or to ontic status at all – be it in the shape of "formal ontology", of "regional ontology", of *Seinssinn* or of eidetic being in general – should be interpreted in the *operative* rather than in the thematic context.

The concept of ontology, however latent in Husserl's thinking, serves more as an operative shade, a medium of understanding, through which he seeks to arrive at the fundamental theme of his philosophy, viz., transcendental subjectivity. Nevertheless there remains always a tension, as it were, between the operative presupposition of thinking and the theme itself just because the operative concepts themselves in their turn seek to be thematised. On the one hand, the concept of being serves merely as an operative medium for formulating the central theme of philosophy; on the other hand, there is a drive for the concept itself to be asserted as the theme. Consequently, an unresolved opposition between these two directions of the concept – and in the long run this hidden dialectic does remain within phenomenological philosophy.

Another criterion of the ontological standpoint is still worth considering in this context. In adopting an ontology we cannot remain accepting at a distance a merely *possible* way of looking at things. To accept it would mean committing oneself not only to a particular doctrine of being but to a basic conceptual scheme, by reference to which all experience, even the most commonplace one, could be – or rather should be – interpreted. Does phenomenology promise, if not definitely posit, such a conceptual scheme? The question could perhaps be met with an unambiguous "no", had not Husserl later brought the phenomenological philosophy to a near-speculative phase – at least in his last work, *Die Krisis etc.* But in the latter he does exhibit a culminating tendency towards a *teleological* outlook – the "telos" inherent in the rational essence of man, who exercises self-understanding *(Selbstverständnis)* – as the natural outcome of a thoroughgoing constitutive phenomenology.[12] At that stage the key notion is that of "accomplishing subjectivity" *(leistende Subjektivität)*, which proves in the long run to be "world-constituting", and earns accordingly even the title of "absolute subjectivity".

Indeed Husserl further refers to the "necessary concrete way of being" *(Seinsweise)* as pertaining to such subjectivity; and the highest task of philosophy, he declares, is to discover that way of being in a transcendental life *(transzendentales Leben)* of world-constitution *(Weltkonstitution)* – a discovery which should impart a new meaning to our natural understanding of the world.[13] Further there seems apparently to be a positively metaphysical strain present in Husserlian thinking, when he even choses to characterize this so-called "transcendental life" as "immortal".[14] But such characterization, it should be remembered, need not be taken as a metaphysical assertion; it is rather to be taken as a statement concerning the phenomenologically inescapable status of transcendental subjectivity. As Husserl states it quite categorically, for the transcendental original life *(das transzendentale urtümliche Leben)*, to perish would bear no meaning – *"es ist 'unsterblich', weil das Sterben dafür keinen Sinn hat"*. This basic phenomenological assertion should not as such be mistaken for a piece of speculative metaphysics concerning transcendent realities.

The way to assess such apparently metaphysical trends would again be to rightly comprehend the methodological approach, in terms of which a total view of things could possibly be attempted, at least schematically – even from a phenomenological standpoint. Transcendental subjectivity no doubt appears to be promoted to the level of a principle, which alone provides the key to all world-explanation, beginning right from the level of common pre-scientific experience (what Husserl would denote by the expression *"Lebenswelt")*. But even that position would be far from deriving a self-complete conceptual scheme out of a fixed ontology and fitting all aspects of experience, even the trivial, to the all-comprehensive scheme of explanation obtained thereby.

---

[12] Cf. *Krisis*, § 73.
[13] *Ibid.*, p. 275.
[14] Cf. Husserl's *Manuskript*, k III 6.

At most (or at its worst!) phenomenology could be spoken of as losing itself in a system of near-teleological explanation, at the centre of which stands the foundational principle of transcendental subjectivity. But such being the case, the progress of phenomenology would be rather in a reverse direction. Thus its procedure is not to start with an accepted view of being, even though latent, but to trace the essentialities behind the neutralized presentations in consciousness, taking the cue with the pre-reflective world of common experience. And the whole line of enquiry tends to fall back on the unfailingly "operative" principle that is transcendental subjectivity. As to the latter, of course, the lasting predicament of the phenomenologist would be there – the crux upon which phenomenological philosophy is bound to stumble again and again. And perhaps it can maintain itself unhurt through all this stumbling.

VII

From our preceding discussions it may now appear evident that in taking a fuller estimate of the phenomenological philosophy, an element of "ontological promise" can hardly be dispensed with. But that pertains to the very nature of phenomenology itself, and need not be considered as something over and above its methodological outlook. The possibility of ontological horizons remains an open one – as unactualized possibles, not as actualities. As in the context of his philosophy of logic in particular,[15] Husserl does leave some room for "ontological attitude" *(ontologische Einstellung)* – one which is a theoretically possible attitude, but not necessarily in disjunction with the phenomenological one. Phenomenological or transcendental-subjective attitude *may* combine with the ontological one – or even may not. And the latter choice need not affect the genuine character of phenomenology, so long as the latter decides to remain primarily a methodological program of analysis of experience, a critique of consciousness.

In assessing Husserl's genuine standpoint, we might even go a

---

[15] *Form. u. tr. Logik*, § 41.

step further and maintain that Husserl actually goes "beyond metaphysics". One could speak of metaphysics within the framework of phenomenology only so far as that concerns the foundation not of being but of *knowing*. As Thévenaz remarks, "Metaphysics is radically transcended in a metanoetics".[16] On final analysis, phenomenology does remain a search – and an open one – for the conditions of the possibility of knowledge and experience. Whatever theory of being seem to be involved in such an investigation, it can at best be *shown* (somewhat in a Wittgensteinian sense) as a possible one, but not prescribed as a doctrine. And the distinction between "description" and "prescription" is one that can hardly be resolved in the long run. For the distinction is even more basic than merely a functional one.

Taking all these points into consideration, one is almost prompted to pose the image of a rope-walker, keeping his balance, as it were, on the tight rope – the rope, namely, of phenomenological neutrality. Loyal to experience, the rope-walker makes his cautious way on the sharp edge lying between the two poles of naturalistic belief on the one hand and ontological commitment on the other.

[16] Thévenaz, p. 148.

CHAPTER VIII

CONCLUSION

From our foregoing essays certain issues emerge, which may be noted in conclusion as follows.

1. Phenomenology offers a new methodology in philosophical investigations; and the approach is as much non-empirical as non-metaphysical. For the rationale of the approach is the attempt at relating experience and transcendence. The method of phenomenological investigations departs both from the usual philosophic method of logical deduction as well as from scientific method.

1.1 The method of reasoning usually employed in philosophical enquiry can broadly be characterized as logico-deductive. And in this context the claim of formal logic – in the traditional as well as modern sense – would necessarily arise. So we have considered a critical estimate of formal logic from the phenomenological point of view (See Ch. III) – its inadequacy to serve as the right vehicle of philosophical investigations. In the reasoning of traditional metaphysics we come across transcendent, i.e., empirically non-verifiable, concepts which claim to hold good of facts of experience. These concepts – or definitional statements relating to these concepts – are used in the traditional objective-metaphysical reasoning as logically entailing certain empirical propositions.

1.2 Such a procedure arbitrarily from certain concepts or statements thereof – which are otherwise posed as logically transparent – to the realm of facts should prove to be rather dogmatic in the matter of interpretation of experience. This is how an objective aprioristic metaphysics would proceed. But here the very aim of understanding the presuppositional concepts in relation to experience – i.e., as holding good of experience

– is not to be met. In other words, this approach fails to meet the said problem of experience and transcendence.

1.3 Coming to the sphere of natural science too, we observe a procedure largely sharing in common the traditional method of philosophizing, viz. the logico-deductive method. Only scientific method has to combine logical deduction with formulation of hypothesis and empirical verification. The hypothetico-deductive method of science is aimed at the objective determination of relations among facts or groups of facts, or between laws and facts. But in science the necessity of the conclusion, pertaining to empirical generalizations concerned, is obtained altogether in an objective direction – independent of being related to the knowing function as such. Consequently the connection between data and any conclusion based on them is not understood as constituted by the subjective operation of passing from data to conclusion.

2.1 The inadequacy of the common logical method and/or scientific method brings phenomenology to a different approach in the matter of relating presuppositions to experience. This alternative approach proceeds *to* presuppositions rather than *from* them. Accordingly the presuppositions of knowledge and experience – those that make knowledge and experience possible – are themselves sought to be traced back. And the process of tracing out the presuppositions should begin right from the level of experience as given. Consequently a new level of reasoning seems to emerge – sharply differentiated from the traditional formal-objective logic. This is what we have considered to be the other logic proposed by Husserl, viz., "transcendental logic". (See Ch. III).[1]

2.2 Now, the common logical relation of implication or entailment cannot be regarded as equivalent to the supposed relation obtaining between ideal presuppositions and the experience manifold, with respect to which they are the presuppositions or conditions of possibility. Of course, in case of a set of premises entailing a conclusion, the former can be spoken of as presuppositions with reference to the latter. But there we start with premises, the presuppositional character of which is clearly determined only

---

[1] Also cf. Author's article "On Transcendental Method": in *The Philosophical Quarterly*, January 1965 (India).

with reference to the conclusion following from them.

2.3 In tracing presuppositions out of experience, we have to start, on the other hand, not with presuppositions themselves but rather with the given, of which the former are the implicates. In a sense we start with the conclusion in the shape of the given in experience, and move backwards to the premises, as it were, out of which such conclusion, i.e., given objectivity, could possibly follow. The procedure may well be characterized as "inverted inference". Of course, even this characterization would prove to be somewhat misleading. For, either logical inference moves on fact level, which is common to data and conclusion alike; or it operates purely on the level of symbolic forms. In case of the proposed method, on the other hand, what is intended is a passage from facts as given to non-factual essentialities.[2]

3.1 In the phenomenological approach the emphasis is evidently shifted from a mere formal analysis and deduction, external to experience, to reflective analysis effected in the direction of meaning consciousness itself. What Kant calls "transcendental reflection", as distinct from "logical reflection",[3] here comes into view. According to Kant, logical reflection is the mere act of comparison of the given representations, taking no account of the corresponding faculty of knowledge to which such representations originally belong. Transcendental reflection, on the other hand, is directed to the ground on which the objective comparison of representations with each other is possible. As such, it cannot be regarded as belonging to the same faculty of knowing as logical reflection. What such reflection implies in respect of judgment is a distinguishment of the cognitive faculty (*Unterscheidung der Erkenntniskraft*) to which the given concepts belong.[4] This same principle of distinguishment is in broad followed in the method of phenomenological reduction too, so far as the latter seeks to trace back the given representations to the respective faculties of origination.

3.2 This line of reasoning – to use the term "reasoning" not in its narrower sense of mere formal-deductive and/or inductive reasoning – tends to view the conclusion as the internal root of

[2] *Ibid.*
[3] Vide *Kritik der reinen Vernunft*, Elementarlehre, II. Teil, I. Abt., II. Buch, Anhang.
[4] *Ibid.*

the data. That means that the given manifold (which in a way serves as conclusion) is to be viewed as rooted in consciousness intending objectivity; and such comprehension could be possible through a methodological subjective deepening of the data.[5] So to put the rationale of the so-called "transcendental logic" in phenomenological terms, logical forms are to be interpreted in the light of the functionality of consciousness generating the ways of givenness pertaining to logical forms. This givenness in meaning consciousness is alone to be regarded as constituting the said evidence, on the ground of which these idealities can be posited. Accordingly the "original constitution" in the evidence-functionality of consciousness is looked upon by Husserl as the foundation of the ideal objectivity pertaining to logical forms and universals of thought.

3.3 This epistemologico-genetic approach to thought structure brings phenomenological intuitionism fully into play. Husserl puts the central point of intuitionism direct when he declares: Knowledge is insight *(Erkenntnis ist Einsicht)*.[6] Shorn of construction, shorn of hypostatization, knowledge, on ultimate analysis, is born of intuition. This rootedness in intuition alone would impart to knowledge its character of evident truth and certainty. But the said insights or intuitions, which have value in themselves *(Selbstwert)*, are by no means to be looked upon as mere fleeting acts of introspection.[7]

3.4 Nor does phenomenological intuitionism in any case involve mysticism.[8] Such intuitionism does not suggest a surrender of rational investigations in favour of an alogism of some kind – be it Bergsonian anti-intellectualism or Existentialistic irrationalism or religious mysticism in broad. For phenomenology remains first and last interested in the explanation of knowledge in the clarification of the foundations of science. The phenomenological philosophy of science, as we have considered – like the transcendental logic itself – seeks to turn the genesis of evidence

---

[5] Cf. An Indian author, Prof. K. C. Bhattacharyya, prefers to explain the Kantian transcendental method as "a specific experimentation with the subjective level of knowing". Vide Bhattacharyya, *Studies in Philosophy*, Vol. II (14-Appendix).

[6] *Ideen* III, p. 96.

[7] Cf. "Einsicht" heisst dabei mehr als der flüchtige Akt des Einsehens". – *ibid.* (footnote).

[8] Cf. "Aber freilich darf der Intuitionismus nicht in Mystizismus ausschlagen", *Ibid.*

in sciences into respective systems of intelligible knowledge. Even when Husserl refers to pure consciousness – virtually the "first principle" in phenomenological explanation, being itself phenomenologically not further reducible – as "the wonder of all wonder", he at the same time observes that the alleged "miracle" would no longer persist as it becomes subject to the essence-wise analysis of phenomenology. What may initially appear to be a "miracle" proves, on closer study, to be "the problematic within the framework of science" *(das Problematische in der Gestalt wissenschaftlicher Probleme)*, and consequently as comprehensible *(ein Begreifliches)* – whereas a so-called "miracle" is admittedly incomprehensible.[9]

4.1 The introduction of "intuition" in the phenomenological context may, however, seem to approximate to the recognition of "rational intuition" in the Rationalist philosophy. There would perhaps remain little distinction in respect of the fundamental character of the faculty of immediate presentation as between the Cartesian *"clara et distincta perceptio"* and the *Wesensanschauung* (or *Wesensschau)* of phenomenology.[10] Of course, in point of metaphysical nature and status of the contents concerned, the two philosophies would sharply differ. Here again the phenomenological approach in terms of analysis of essence comes very near to the Kantian method of "transcendental reflection". As Kant states it, *reflection (reflexio)* does not concern itself with objects themselves with a view to deriving concepts directly from them, but seeks to discover the subjective conditions under which we can arrive at concepts. In that way the given representations are sought to be related to the different sources of knowledge *(Erkenntnisquellen)*.[11]

4.2 The task of phenomenological investigations – whether in respect of ordinary experience or of scientific knowledge, or in whatever other spheres of human discipline – is to trace back concepts to their corresponding essence-origins, as shown in course of our preceding essays. For, phenomenologically speaking, there should be an essence corresponding to a concept – *"dem*

---

[9] Vide *Ideen III*, p. 75.

[10] Although in a different context, Husserl has admitted a point of agreement with older rationalists, namely, that "an infinity of possibilities precedes actuality" – and consequently, the knowledge of the former precedes that of the latter. *Ibid.*, p. 56.

[11] Kant, *op. cit.*

Begriff entspricht . . . ein Wesen".[12] In this sense phenomenology offers to be the "doctrine of essence" *(Wesenslehre)* – the doctrine that is based on essences rather than one *about* them.

4.3 To be the doctrine of essences *(Wesenslehre)*, concerned with the analysis and description of essences, does not, however, mean that phenomenology stands merely an empirical-descriptive doctrine. As Husserl repeatedly stresses, phenomenology – though *Wesenslehre* – should not be taken as a mere empirical-descriptive theory of essence. For an empirical description of the essences or experience in the empirical context of given facts is not by itself competent to yield a law concerning essence on the level of idealities (or ideal possibilities of experience).[13] Moreover, even in non-empirical description of essences, Phenomenology seems to combine description with analysis – its *modus operandi* is description by analysis.

4.4 The peculiar non-empirical yet non-discursive mode of analysis, in the shape of intuitionism characteristic of phenomenology, seems to incorporate the respective elements of empiricism and rationalism. Even the so-called ordinary language approach (in contemporary linguistic or analytic philosophy) need not be treated as impervious to the method of phenomenological analysis (See Ch. II). A reference may in this connection be made to Austin's use of the expression "linguistic phenomenology" – in the sense of "a sharpened awareness of words to sharpen our perception of, though not as the final arbiter of, the phenomena".[14] Here Austin – an analyst though he is – eventually recognizes at least the need and the possibility of a subjectively deeper analysis of words and their linguistic meaning. So far as phenomenology goes; it would not confine its task to the determination of language use *(Sprachgebrauch)*; it seeks, on the contrary, to bring out a noematic essence as the true meaning behind the bare meaning of a word *(Wortbedeutung)*.[15] (See. Ch. II).

5.1 The possibility, as shown above, of a phenomenological orientation of linguistic analysis only points to the universal

---

[12] *Ideen III*, p. 100.
[13] "Wesensbeschreibung gibt an sich noch kein Wesensgesetz". *Ibid.*, p. 69.
[14] J. L. Austin, *Philosophical Papers*, 6, p. 130.
[15] *Ideen III*, p. 100.

scope of the phenomenological method in the task of conceptual clarification – not only in respect of scientific concepts and theories but also of ordinary experience. Here the question can hardly be avoided – as Prof. Landgrebe, for instance, has appropriately raised it[16] – whether the phenomenological inquiry, constituted as it is, should exclude metaphysics altogether. If the phenomenological critique of experience be concerned with "clarity rather than profundity", how far then should it be removed from a metaphysical system of truths? The answer may be offered in terms of a third alternative (between metaphysics and no metaphysics) in the shape of what Strawson designates, in the context of ordinary language philosophy, as "descriptive metaphysics".[17] It indicates that form of metaphysics which (as distinguished from "revisionary metaphysics") is "content to describe the actual structure of our thought about the world". Like "descriptive metaphysics", phenomenology too is concerned with the most general and fundamental categories and concepts – their interconnexions, and the structure that they form.

5.2 But phenomenology inevitably entails, at certain critical stages of its procedure – even as a non-metaphysical critique of experience – the question of ontological priority, in a way which the analytically-oriented "descriptive metaphysics" of Strawson would not. The crux of the problem in this regard concerns the phenomenological view of consciousness (see Chs. IV and VII); the question of ontological commitment inevitably comes up in respect of the latter. But the question may possibly be met at two levels – either the level of pre-reflective immediacy (i.e., of *Lebenswelt*) or the higher level of pure consciousness, that is the absolute precondition of all constitution of objectivity. At both the levels a purely phenomenological assertion of subjectivity tends almost inevitably towards some sort of *existentialistic* solution. The higher level, however, seems to incline towards a metaphysics of "absolute" consciousness. But the latter, it may be admitted, would be phenomenologically unintelligible, except of course as a "demand" arising out of phenomenological analysis itself – a "metaphysical demand", but not a hypostatized con-

---

[16] L. Landgrebe, "Phenomenology and Metaphysics", in *Philosophy and Phenomenological Research*, Dec. 1949.
[17] P. F. Strawson, *Individuals: An Essay in Descriptive Metaphysics*, Introduction.

cept as such. Turning, on the other hand, to the primary level of
Lebenswelt, consciousness at that stage remains in an undefined
obscure state.

5.3 On final analysis, Husserl takes the concept of "life" as
something primordial and rudimentary. That also imparts a
rudimentary character to subjectivity itself; for the latter, in its
primary phase, finds its place in life – it is one with the experience
that is lived. With Husserl, life is not a "vitalistic" concept nor a
"limiting concept" for intelligent analysis (i.e., unamenable to
intellectual analysis). On the contrary, the stratum of life provides the home for all forms and apriorities, which subsequently
prevail in the realm of science and knowledge at large. Indeed
it has not been so much of a problem for phenomenology to find
the locus of the *a priori*, for the latter is recognized to be originally
grounded in *Lebenswelt*. The formal hypostatized constructions of
a priori concept and propositions originate admittedly out of the
apriorities pertaining to *Lebenswelt* – *lebensweltliches Apriori*.[18]

5.4 The recognition of the formal-general structures of the
Lebenswelt brings into relief the essence of phenomenological continuity. Phenomenologically considered, there need not be any
discontinuity between the level of common experience and that
of scientific knowledge or conceptual thinking. For both of them
alike – and eventually, the possible intermediate stages of half-
theoretic half-scientific knowledge – reveal *a priori* features and
generalities, only more or less explicitly. Such continuity, in

---

[18] Cf. *Krisis*, § 36, p. 143.

N.B. *Lebenswelt* is the primary spatio-temporal world of objects, so far as we experience that in our prescientific (and extrascientific) life of pure experience. But
with all its immediacy and relativity – i.e., reference to subjective experience –
Lebenswelt is still not lacking in its universal structure. For even this rudimentary
world of experience *(Erfahrungswelt)* may reveal, on closer examination, certain
basic features in common – though implicitly – such as causality, spatiality etc.
(see Ch. VI, 6). Husserl even contents that this primary world partakes basically of
the same structures as the world of objective sciences. All "objective apriorities" –
i.e., those pertaining to positive sciences – can necessarily be traced back to the
corresponding apriorities of *Lebenswelt*. Through tracing back the foundational relations in which scientific concepts are rooted in *Lebenswelt*, the functional ground of
validity *(Geltungsfundierung)* of the conceptual constructions of science is obtained.
Ibid.
Following this line of thinking, Husserl further refers to a possible "Ontology of the
Lebenswelt", which should grow purely out of the world of experience – out of pure
evidence obtained in the latter. This proposed "ontology" would be based on the
universal "ground" *(Boden)* of prescientific experience, on which all sciences build
their superstructures. *Ibid.* § 51.

its turn, ensures the possibility of retracing the origin of different conceptual constructs, pertaining to different sciences, through the method of phenomenological reduction.

6.1 As already observed on earlier occasions, behind the phenomenological type of intuitionism (which can as well be characterized as "transcendental empiricism" – see Ch. I, 3.4), the phenomenological philosophy of Husserl exhibits, in its culminating phase, a latent tendency towards "rationalism". The possible origin of this drive, however implicit, towards the conception of an absolute rational order and teleology is not far to seek. For the very concept of subjectivity as foundational and as constitutive of all meaning of objectivity – that is, *leistende Subjektivität* – represents nothing but a universal principle of world-explanation. To such principle nothing is to remain opaque in the light of essence-analysis, no "mystery" – and that assures the claim of a thoroughly *scientific* procedure. This leads Husserl in the long run to recognize the triumph of *reason (Vernunft)* in the universal range of phenomenological explanation.[19] Indeed he goes even so far as to characterize philosophy itself as "rationalism" *(Rationalismus)*, which seeks to proceed in different steps of unfoldment of the reason innate in mankind.[20]

6.2 This "rationalistic" trend seems to be particularly explicit in the Husserlian conception of self-consciousness *(Selbstbesinnung)* in the context of the life of a person *qua person*. (See Ch. V, 5). From the point of view of self-consciousness Husserl distinguishes two stages in personal being. One pertains to the person, who has not yet accomplished the ultimate act of self-consciousness, and the other results from this act. Through the latter alone man attains the ideal level of manhood.[21] The highest function of personhood accordingly lies in that man develops a personal and all-embracing "autonomy". For individual men it signifies the free urge to be oneself as a rational I-principle. On the plane of collective life, again, this would mean the "autonomy of reason"

---

[19] Accordingly Husserl's definition of the so-called "transcendental life" – the ideal goal of phenomenological reflection – as the "life in apodicticity" *(Leben in der Apodiktizität)*. Vide *Krisis*, § 73.

[20] Cf. Husserl, "Die Idee einer philosophischen Kultur", *Erste Philosophie*, I. Teil, Abhandlung.

[21] *Krisis*, p. 486.

(Vernunftautonomie), which may serve as the highest principle of culture.[22]

6.3 This evident acceptance of what seems to be a rationalistic belief in the final phase of phenomenology does not, however, appear to be well-grounded. All that a phenomenological procedure, strictly speaking, could justify may perhaps best be regarded as a "demand" for a metaphysical status of transcendental subjectivity. The principle for world-explanation, itself not further analysable, may well present a "demand" – somewhat in the sense of "ought-to-be".[23]

6.4 The only other metaphysical vindication possible might be obtained at the primary level of *Lebenswelt*. But even the so-called "ontology of *Lebenswelt*" would proceed, after all, in terms of apriorities, however implicit they may otherwise be. And that may well provide the key to a rationalistic world-orientation. The only limiting consideration in this regard might be presented in the form of strict methodological approach of phenomenology.

Taking fully into consideration the typical methodological standpoint of phenomenology – which distinguishes it preeminently from other philosophies – we need not, on ultimate analysis, expect from it further than a kind of "descriptive metaphysics". The position of Platonism, deriving the empirical order from the transcendent order of being, is reversed in this sort of metaphysics; and the point of reference is here directed to the structure of experience itself. The system of truths – of idealities – is sought to be obtained out of the stratum of experience (as lived), but not vice versa. Consequently, what in the long run remains is an *open* system of truths, and not a closed one.

---

[22] Cf. "Die Idee einer phil. Kultur" etc.

[23] Husserl uses the expression "*Sein-sollen*" (i.e., ought-to-be) at least on one occasion – namely, with reference to the essential being of man *(Menschsein)*, conceived as a "teleological being" in view of his capacity for self-consciousness. Cf. *Krisis*, p. 275.

BIBLIOGRAPHY

I. Works of Husserl

Cartesianische Meditationen und Pariser Vorträge. Edited by S. Strasser (Husserliana I). The Hague: Martinus Nijhoff, 1950.

Cartesian Meditations. Translated by Dorion Cairns. The Hague: Martinus Nijhoff, 1960.

"Entwurf einer 'Vorrede' zu den 'Logischen Untersuchungen' (1913)". Edited by Eugen Fink, *Tijdschrift voor Philosophie*, I (1939), pp. 106–133; 319–339.

Erfahrung und Urteil. Untersuchungen zur Genealogie der Logik. Edited by Ludwig Landgrebe. Hamburg: Claassen, 3rd edition, 1964.

Erste Philosophie (1923/24). Erster Teil: Kritische Ideengeschichte. Edited by Rudolf Boehm (Husserliana VII). The Hague: Martinus Nijhoff, 1956.

Erste Philosophie (1923/24). Zweiter Teil: Theorie der phänomenologischen Reduktion. Edited by Rudolf Boehm (Husserliana VIII). The Hague: Martinus Nijhoff, 1959. – Cf. also the *Abhandlung* "Meditation über die Idee eines individuellen und Gemeinschaftslebens in absoluter Selbstverantwortung", *ibid.*, pp. 193–202.

Formale und transzendentale Logik. Versuch einer Kritik der logischen Vernunft. Halle a.S.: Max Niemeyer, 1929.

Ideas: General Introduction to Pure Phenomenology. Translation of *Ideen I* by W. R. Boyce Gibson. London: George Allen and Unwin, 1931.

Die Idee der Phänomenologie. Fünf Vorlesungen. Edited by Walter Biemel (Husserliana II). The Hague: Martinus Nijhoff, 2nd. edition, 1958.

"Die Idee einer philosophischen Kultur", *Japanisch-deutsche Zeitschrift für Wissenschaft und Technik*, I (1923). Also in *Erste Philosophie*, vol. I, pp. 203–207.

Ideen zu einer reinen Phänomenologie und phänomenologischen Philosophie. Erstes Buch: Allgemeine Einführung in die reine Phänomenologie. Edited by Walter Biemel (Husserliana III). The Hague: Martinus Nijhoff, 1950.

Ideen zu einer reinen Phänomenologie und phänomenologischen Philosophie. Zweites Buch: Phänomenologische Untersuchungen zur Konstitution. Edited by Marly Biemel (Husserliana IV). The Hague: Martinus Nijhoff, 1952.

Ideen zu einer reinen Phänomenologie und phänomenologischen Philosophie. Drittes Buch: Die Phänomenologie und die Fundamente der Wissenschaften.

Edited by Marly Biemel (Husserliana V). The Hague: Martinus Nijhoff, 1952.

Die Krisis der europäischen Wissenschaften und die transzendentale Phänomenologie. Eine Einleitung in die phänomenologische Philosophie. Edited by Walter Biemel (Husserliana VI). The Hague: Martinus Nijhoff, 1954.

Logische Untersuchungen. Erster Band: Prolegomena zur reinen Logik. Halle a.S.: Max Niemeyer, 1900. Second revised edition: Halle a.S.: Max Niemeyer, 1913.

Logische Untersuchungen. Zweiter Band: Untersuchungen zur Phänomenologie und Theorie der Erkenntnis. Halle a.S.: Max Niemeyer, 1901. Second revised edition in two parts, with the following subtitles: *Zweiter Band: Untersuchungen zur Phänomenologie und Theorie der Erkenntnis,* I. Teil. Halle a.S.: Max Niemeyer, 1913. *Zweiter Band: Elemente einer phänomenologischen Aufklärung der Erkenntnis,* II. Teil. Halle a.S.: Max Niemeyer, 1921.

"Nachwort zu meinen "Ideen zu einer reinen Phänomenologie und phänomenologischen Philosophie'," *Jahrbuch für Philosophie und phänomenologische Forschung,* XI, 1930.

Phänomenologische Psychologie. Vorlesungen Sommersemester 1925. Edited by Walter Biemel (Husserliana IX). The Hague: Martinus Nijhoff, 1962.

"Phenomenology", *Encyclopaedia Britannica,* 14th edition, 1927, vol. 17.

"Philosophie als strenge Wissenschaft", *Logos,* I, (1910/11), pp. 289–341.

Philosophie der Arithmetik. Psychologische und logische Untersuchungen. Vol. I. Halle a.S.: C. E. M. Pfeffer, 1891.

II. Unpublished Manuscripts of Husserl

The use of the manuscripts referred to and cited in this work was made possible through the kind co-operation of the Husserl-Archiv of Cologne, where I was allowed to make use of the unpublished materials. The numbers of the Mss. here cited are in accordance with the transcriptions of the same in Husserl-Archiv, Köln.

Ms. A V 7 (1920–32) Wesensform der Personalität – Anthropologie. Personale Lebenswelt – Naturale Einstellung. Zweiseitigkeit.

Ms. A VI 15 (1929) Der Mensch als Thema – Seele – Geisteswissenschaft.

Ms. A VI 21 (1928–33) Die Welt und die Kausalität – die induktive Äußerlichkeit.

Ms. K III 6 (1934–36) Without title.

Ms. M I 1 (1917) Phänomenologie und Erkenntnistheorie für Anfänger.

III. Other References

Austin, J. L., *Philosophical Papers*, Oxford, Clarendon, 1961.

Ayer, A. J. (ed.), *Logical Positivism*. Introduction by Ayer, Glencoe, Free Press, 1959.

Bhattacharyya, K. C., *Studies in Philosophy*, Vols. I and II. Progressive Publishers, Calcutta, 1956 and 1958.

Biemel, W., "Husserls Encyclopaedia-Britannica-Artikel und Heideggers Anmerkungen dazu", *Tijdschrift voor Philosophie*, XII, (1950), pp. 246–280.

Farber, M., *The Foundation of Phenomenology. Edmund Husserl and the Quest for a Rigorous Science of Philosophy*, Cambridge: Harvard University Press, 1943.

Farber, M., "Experience and Transcendence", *Philosophy and Phenomenological Research*, XII, (1951–52), pp. 1–23.

Fink, E., "Die phänomenologische Philosophie Edmund Husserls in der gegenwärtigen Kritik", *Kant-Studien*, XXXIIX, (1933), pp. 319–383.

Fink, E., "Operative Begriffe in Husserls Phänomenologie", *Zeitschrift für philosophische Forschung*, XI, (1957), pp. 321–337.

Gurwitsch, A., "A non-egological Conception of Consciousness", *Philosophy and Phenomenological Research*, I, (1941), pp. 325–338.

Gurwitsch, A., "The Last Work of Edmund Husserl", *Philosophy and Phenomenological Research*, XVI, (1955–56), pp. 380–399; XVII, (1956/57), pp. 370–398.

Heidegger, M., *Sein und Zeit*, Tübingen: Max Niemeyer, 1960.

Kant, I., *Kritik der reinen Vernunft*, Hamburg: Felix Meiner, 1956.

Kaufmann, F., "Phenomenology and Logical Empiricism", *Philosophical Essays in memory of Edmund Husserl*, ed. M. Farber, Cambridge: Harvard Uuniversity Press, 1940.

Landgrebe, L., "Phenomenology and Metaphysics", *Philosophy and Phenomenological Research*, X, (1949/50), pp. 197–205.

Landgrebe, L., "Seinsregionen und regionale Ontologien in Husserls Phänomenologie", *Studium Generale*, IX, (1956), pp. 313–324.

Merleau-Ponty, M., *Phenomenology of Perception*, trans. Colin Smith, Routledge and Kegan Paul, 1962.

Mohanty, J. N., *Edmund Husserl's Theory of Meaning* (Phaenomenologica 14). The Hague: Martinus Nijhoff, 1964.

Quine, W. V. O., *From a Logical Point of View*, Harvard University Press, 1953.

Reichenbach, H., *Modern Philosophy of Science*, Routledge and Kegan Paul, 1959.

Russell, B., *Our Knowledge of the External World*, Allen and Unwin, 1926.

Ryle, G., *Dilemmas*, Cambridge, 1954.

Sartre, J.-P., *The Transcendence of the Ego: An Existentialist Theory of Consciousness*. Translated by F. Williams and R. Kirkpatrick, New York: Noonday Press, 2nd printing, 1959.

Scheler, M., *Der Formalismus in der Ethik und die materiale Wertethik* (Gesammelte Werke, Bd. 2). Bern – München: Franke, 5th edition, 1966.

Sinha, D., "On transcendental method", *The Philosophical Quarterly* (India), 1965, pp. 251–256.

Spiegelberg, H., "How subjective is Phenomenology?", *Proceedings of the American Catholic Philosophical Association*, 1959.

Spiegelberg, H., *The Phenomenological Movement. A Historical Introduction* (Phaenomenologica, voll. 5 and 6). The Hague: Martinus Nijhoff, 2nd edition, 1965.

Strawson, P. F., *Individuals: An Essay in Descriptive Metaphysics*, London: Methuen, 1959.

Thévenaz, P., *What is Phenomenology?* Ed. James M. Edie, Chicago: Quadrangle, 1962.

Urmson, J. O., *Philosophical Analysis*, Oxford: Clarendon, 1956.

Waismann, F., "How I see Philosophy", *Contemporary British Philosophy*, Third Series, Allen and Unwin, Macmillan, 2nd edition, 1961.

Wittgenstein, L., *Philosophical Investigations*, Oxford: Blackwell, 1953.

INDEX